# THE
# STRATEGIC
# INVESTMENT
# DECISION

# THE STRATEGIC INVESTMENT DECISION

◆

## Evaluating Opportunities in Dynamic Markets

◆

ROGER OLDCORN
and
DAVID PARKER

PITMAN PUBLISHING
128 Long Acre, London W.C2E 9AN

A Division of Pearson Professional Limited

First published in Great Britain 1996

© Pearson Professional Limited 1996

*British Library Cataloguing in Publication Data*
A CIP catalogue record for this book can be obtained
from the British Library.

ISBN 0 273 61779 6

1 3 5 7 9 10 8 6 4 2

Typeset by Phoenix Photosetting, Chatham, Kent
Printed and bound in Great Britain by
Biddles Ltd, Guildford and King's Lynn

*The Publishers' policy is to use paper manufactured
from sustainable forests.*

# About the Authors

ROGER OLDCORN is Director of Studies, the Senior Management Programme at Henley Management College, where he also lectures in finance and accounting.

After reading economics at the University of Exeter he worked in the food and hotel industries for a number of years in management accounting and planning functions, before joining the Centre for Interfirm Comparison as Senior Project Manager.

For a few years he worked for the United Nations (UNIDO) based in Vienna, as an expert in industrial performance evaluation and carried out long-term assignments in India and the Middle East. He also lived in the USA based in Milwaukee, Wisconsin, working for an American consultancy company, and entered management education on returning to Britain. Prior to Henley he was Business Development Adviser at Kingston Regional Management Centre (Kingston University).

DAVID PARKER is a chartered accountant who has been involved with management training and consultancy for over twenty-five years. He has degrees in economics and accounting and accounting and finance from Bristol University and the London School of Economics. A member of the Associate Faculty of Henley Management College, he has lectured and written about all aspects of accounting and finance to managers. For a time he lectured in the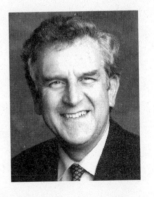

USA at the Wharton School, University of Pennsylvania, before returning to the UK. He has designed and presented courses for business managers in companies such as IBM, Sony, ICL, Shell and British Aerospace. His wide-ranging consultancy experience has been gained from his accountancy practice and his family business – supplier of laboratory equipment to schools and colleges – in which, until recently, he was managing director.

# CONTENTS

◆

# INTRODUCTION

◆

If you want a successful business, you have to look at the long term. Not only do you have to make profits today (to stay in business), but you have to think about how the business is going to make profits tomorrow. The process of thinking about the future of a business enterprise is Strategic Planning and making it happen is Strategic Management. Our concern in this book is to answer the question: "How do successful firms go about choosing effective strategies?" Implicit in this is the related problem of deciding where investment should be made.

The book is designed for managers who have to take strategic investment decisions, often without the benefit of much "expert" help: managers in medium and small firms, and possibly in strategic business units of larger companies, especially where these are decentralized. It is not primarily for corporate planners in head offices. We intend that it will also be of value to students of business administration in the hope that this latter category might be encouraged to study the more specialist textbooks dealing with the different aspects of the subject.

The main focus of this book is to convince the reader that investment decisions in business should only be taken in the context of strategic plans, because we believe that far too much money has been invested in projects over the years which have obviously (with the benefit of perfect hindsight) been wasted. We can all look back and quote examples, both large and small, of firms doing something which has cost a great deal and yet which has turned out to be of no benefit to their owners. Of course many investment decisions are taken with an apparently sound strategic basis; the logic appears impeccable. Yet things go wrong. They do not turn out the way management planned it and the reasons are manifold.

The stimulus and the excitement would be taken out of business if we always knew with certainty what is going to happen in the future.

The fact that we cannot does not validate the excuse that we should not plan, nor analyze, nor evaluate. On the contrary, it seems to us that the more analysis and evaluation that is carried out, the better are the chances of creating a successful strategy. Experts in racing circles study "form" before investing and military leaders study the enemy and the territory before taking decisions about where and when to attack. Similarly in business, study form, and evaluate the territory first. But beyond the analysis and the evaluation and all the costings, two elements are needed. First, the choice of strategic direction is the product of unquantifiable factors such as flair, insight, creativity and intuition. Second, no matter how brilliant the strategy in concept, without appropriate leadership nothing will happen.

The field we are exploring is to some extent well trodden, in the sense that volumes have been written about the mechanics of capital investment techniques and their appraisal. These textbooks, unfortunately often omit the wider managerial and strategic dimension – they assume that whatever project is being evaluated will by definition be a successful addition to the company's portfolio of activities. Such books tend to be written by financial experts. On the other hand, there are also volumes on strategy and there are those would seem to think that strategy formulation is easy; it is a simple matter of looking at the business environment, choosing a novel course of action and just going ahead. If it was so easy and so simple, all big business would be hugely profitable. Our point is that for successful strategic investment decision-making continuously inspired leadership is vital.

Effective strategic investment decision-making is, therefore, not easy because it brings together three very different managerial skills – painstaking analytical skills together with creative skills, and leadership.

We have written the book with both British and American readers particularly in mind. We have used American convention in the accounting sections of the text and hope that the UK reader will be able to "translate" without difficulty. We have also used a mixture of terminology and trust that this will not be confusing. The fact that debtors are receivables and debt is borrowing can be a nice trap for any manager operating transatlantically, as is the "stocks equals inventory equal shares" problem. Also the examples we have choosen are those we know about and we hope that the readers – wherever they are located – will be able to identify with the problems and issues being presented. The global marketplace may be unreal for many, but this should not lead to a parochial attitude of mind.

Of course nothing is new in business theory, and strategy has its roots in war. The soldier and writer von Clausewitz had some interesting things to say about strategy which are worth thinking about even now – getting on for two hundred years later:

> *The means and forms that the strategist employs are so very simple, so familiar from constant repetition, that it seems ridiculous . . . when critics discuss them with ponderous solemnity.*
>
> *It is even more ridiculous when we consider that these critics usually exclude all moral qualities from strategic theory, and only examine material factors. They reduce everything to a few mathematical formulas of equilibrium and superiority, of time and space, limited by a few angles and lines. If that were really all, it would hardly provide a scientific problem for a schoolboy.*
>
> *The relations between material factors are all very simple; what is more difficult to grasp are the intellectual factors involved. Even so, it is only in the highest realms of strategy that intellectual complications and extreme diversity of factors and relationships occur. At that level there is little or no difference between strategy, policy and statesmanship . . . everything in strategy is very simple, but that does not mean that everything is very easy. It takes more strength of will to make an important decision in strategy than in tactics . . . in strategy everything has to be guessed at and presumed.*
>
> Karl Marie von Clausewitz, *On War*, 1833

We hope you will enjoy this book and find the intellectual effort stimulating and sufficiently motivating to persuade you to follow up some of the ideas and also to use the techniques in your own business environment. Have fun – make money.

♦

Every day directors and senior managers of companies have to take decisions about aspects of the business they are running.

♦

# Chapter 1

◆

# WHAT IS CORPORATE STRATEGY?

Every day directors and senior managers of companies have to take decisions about aspects of the business they are running. Many are decisions which will solve a problem, many are concerned with today's business or with the immediate future of the business. A few decisions are investment decisions, where money has to be spent today in the expectation (or hope) that the business will be better off in the future as a result. And of these investment decisions just a few can be termed Strategic Investment Decisions, since the thinking which lies behind them is not operational, nor routine, but long term, entrepreneurial and seeking in some way to significantly improve the company's fortunes. They are about the investment of time, money and energy into a project or venture where the result is unknown because it will happen in the future: it is a risk.

In this chapter we will discuss the nature of strategic investment decisions and look at some of the fundamental issues of Corporate Strategy.

# WHAT IS A STRATEGIC INVESTMENT?

Consider these recent business cases.

### Le Hotel Lièvre Blanc

A British couple decided to buy a small, rundown, old, former coaching inn in the French Alps region in a not too fashionable ski resort. They knew about the hotel business and had always wanted to live in France. The opportunity arose, so they bought. The price? A mere one French franc – but they also took on the responsibility for many thousand francs of debt and the certainty of having to spend a whole lot more renovating the place.

### Marks & Spencer goes East

In March 1995 Marks & Spencer, the British-based retail store group, announced that it was looking to expand in various countries around the world. The stated criterion was to seek sites of about 40,000 sq. ft, with freehold ownership where mass market opportunities exist. The company has added Germany to its list of prospects and is considering various Far Eastern countries, but not Japan – property costs in Tokyo "prohibit decent returns."

### Siemens goes British

In August 1995 Siemens, the giant German electronics company, announced its decision to develop a site on Tyneside in the North-East of England to manufacture microchips "application specific integrated circuits" (Asics) for use with such things as smart cards and mobile phones, at a cost of some £1.13 bn.

These three examples all illustrate aspects of the Strategic Investment Decision. None of the decisions are as simple as they sound – consider them and try to visualize the thinking that lay behind each decision, for in each case the strategic decision is not just one decision but several, each building on the other.

### The hotel

The owners wanted a particular lifestyle and decision number one was to own an hotel in France. Then the decision to take is: where to look? Next the opportunity came up and the decision is now: buy or not? The price was small but the other issues in the equation were huge – for instance:

- Could we attract a sufficiently large clientèle to make enough profit?
- How much of our profit would be taken away by debt interest?
- How much will it cost to redevelop the hotel and its facilities?
- Can we get the staff?

Decisions, decisions.

### Marks & Spencer

The underlying decision here is to accelerate the firm's expansion outside the UK. This is the first part of the strategic decision. The second part is the search for the right conditions. Stage three is the evaluation of the options under apparently strict criteria: to generate a "decent return on the investment." Stage four is "Go for it or not."

### Siemens

The first part of the strategic decision was to grow the business by investing in Asics. How do they know that they can make money out of such devices? The second aspect to this decision is: what capacity should the plant have? This would assume that Siemens can assess how big the market will be and how big a player they want to be in that market.

The next aspect to the decision is location. Apparently three locations were shortlisted: Austria, Ireland, and Tyneside. At this stage the company's decision criteria included more than the cost of building the plant, though the inducements to locate in any of the three locations added to the desirability of going ahead wherever. The other factors included: geologically sound land, availability of skilled labor, first-class international communications facilities, university research capabilities and (surprisingly) abundant water supplies.

All three cases demonstrate the fundamental issues facing senior managers (or owners) of business enterprises:

- How do we secure survival and prosperity?
- In what direction should we go – in product/service terms and in location?
- What are the costs and what are likely yields from the possible options?
- Does our favored solution make sense?
- Are we prepared to take the risk?

# DECISION-MAKING AND THE RATIONAL MANAGER

*Not to decide questions that are not pertinent at the time is uncommon good sense, though to raise them may be uncommon perspicacity.*

(Chester Barnard)

If all managers were rational all of the time, they would always follow a logical sequence of actions whenever a decision had to be taken and the sequence is often referred to as the *Six-Step Approach*. The steps are:

## 1 Define the objective

Under this heading the questions to be asked include:

- What are we trying to achieve?
- What is the aim of the exercise?

- What problem are we trying to solve (assuming, of course, we recognize we have a problem)?

In business strategy terms we will look later at the types of strategic objective which might crop up, but a simple example illustrates the point.

---

### The Hotstuff Spice Works (1)

There was once a small family business importing, processing, and selling spices. The processing and packaging technology was not complex and the firm became very successful, growing sales until it was working two full shifts, six days a week.
The problem is not hard to identify:

- Do we allow the business to grow more?

or even more fundamentally

- Do we want to grow the business?

---

## 2 Collect information

This step in the process is called fact-finding, but also includes analysis – the process of looking at facts and at statistics to try to get a better feeling of the nature of the problem and of the issues surrounding it.

---

### The Hotstuff Spice Works (2)

The information needed here was factual in part and would include:

- How much would a new plant cost to build and install? How quickly?
- What costs would be incurred in, say, doubling output?

Other information would be harder to find:

- Where does the money come from?
- Could the additional output be sold and where? Who would buy?
- Have we got, or could we obtain, the right people?

---

In strategy terms, the difficulty lies not so much in gathering information about the past or even the present, but about the future, where everything is about *prediction*.

## 3 Develop some solutions

In an ideal word, all the possible courses of action would be set out – much like in a race where all the runners are listed and if you want to gamble, all the facts about each runner are set out.

In strategy there is no preset list of runners. These have to be developed and some creative thinking is needed to come up with a good list of alternatives. Also the longer you think about the problem and discuss it, more and more alternative actions will present themselves – until exhaustion overtakes you.

> **In strategy there is no preset list of runners. These have to be developed and some creative thinking is needed to come up with a good list of alternatives.**

---

**The Hotstuff Spice Works (3)**

The options for growth included:

- Do nothing
- Buy a competitor
- Build a new plant (if so where and what size)
- Subcontract some processes
- Go into a joint venture or even a strategic alliance.

---

## 4 Evaluate

Stage three does not evaluate: it is more of a list – possibly brainstormed – of the most obvious courses of action to take. These need then to be costed out, just as in a horse race all the facts are presented about each runner, so that an intelligent assessment can be made of the likely winner. On top of the facts, each horse's chances of winning are given: the odds are a calculation of the probability of success. Unfortunately in business strategy, the odds for each alternative strategic action are not easily calculated and indeed the "facts" may be no more than intelligent guesswork. The options can be placed on a scale:

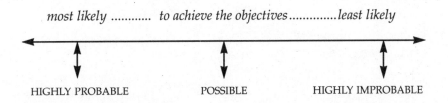

*most likely* ............ *to achieve the objectives* ..............*least likely*

HIGHLY PROBABLE       POSSIBLE       HIGHLY IMPROBABLE

### The Hotstuff Spice Works (4)

The questions asked of each of the alternative courses of action included:

- What will it cost?
- How much profit will be generated?
- What is the timing of the cash flows?
- How long will it last?
- What are the "odds?"

And underlying all these: does it meet our objective?

## 5 Choose

Arguably the hardest part of decision-making is actually choosing the course of action to take. Sometimes the right course of action is obvious, but often the choice is between options which are not perfect, but which will have some "good" features and some less desirable characteristics. In horse racing some gamblers always back the favourite, others back "form," while others back the jockey. All are following "decision rules" to help them decide.

The decision in strategy planning can be taken by following a set of decision rules and as we shall see, this can lead to second-best decisions. Ideally, all the options are gradually sifted, so that in the end the action taken is the best action, *having regard to the aims of the exercise*. The snag is that all this takes time and if care is not taken, the decision is too late – or if left too long – some of the options get eliminated by external factors and not by choice.

> **Ideally, all the options are gradually sifted, so that in the end the action taken is the best action, *having regard to the aims of the exercise.***

---

### The Hotstuff Spice Works (5)

It was decided that the best option was to buy a competitor. The cost was higher than the build option but quicker, and moreover a lot more secure than the joint venture or subcontracting. Unfortunately, the firm dithered over the decision and the company that had been interested in selling out went to another rival. By now, build was the only action left

## 6 Take action

It may seem obvious, but there is no point in taking a decision unless action is immediately taken to make it happen. With strategic decisions, making things happen usually involves many people over a period of time which can extend over many years. The skill of the strategic manager is that of ensuring that once the decision is taken, all who are going to be involved need to be clear about what is expected, the timing of events and the financial implications of the whole exercise. If (as is often the case) some persuasion is needed, the skill of the manager in implementing change becomes as important as the decision itself. There is no point deciding on some grand strategy if nobody is in favor of the idea. It is in this context that the manager's role as leader is most needed.

> **There is no point deciding on some grand strategy if nobody is in favor of the idea. It is in this context that the manager's role as leader is most needed.**

# ANATOMY OF A STRATEGIC DECISION

## The Troll gas field

In May 1995 a huge gas field platform was towed into the North Sea from Norway and installed in 303 m of water to extract and pipe gas back into Europe. The field was discovered in 1979 by Shell Norway and contains an estimated 1,250 bn cu m of gas – enough to supply 10 percent of Europe's gas needs for the next 50 years. The overall cost of the investment – platform, pipelines, and onshore processing plant – is **US$ 4.67 billion**. The platform is the biggest concrete structure in the world, some 472 m high and weighing over one million tonnes.

Apart from the enormity of the Troll project – being described as the "Eighth Wonder of the World" – it is a fascinating example of the Strategic Investment Decision in action. To spend such a large sum of money is by any standard remarkable and Shell must be confident of the field's ability to generate enough cash over a sufficiently long period of time to give the company's shareholders sufficient reward for the risk. So what are the questions that will have been asked before the decision was taken? They would have included:

- Are we sure the reserves are big enough to justify the costs of extraction?
- Are we sure of the quality of gas?
- Can we operate in a hostile environment in over 300 m of water, with 30 m waves, and over 65 km from shore?
- Are there unacceptable environmental risks?
- What price can we get for the gas we extract?
- How much will it cost to get the gas to the customer?
- Will there be a profit if the price of gas falls by 20 percent or 50 percent or 80 percent and what are the chances of gas prices falling?

- Overall, are the risks of *not* producing a reasonable return on the investment at an acceptable level? (or another way – are the odds in favour of success short enough?).

- Are there better things we could do with the money?

It can readily be seen that the decision is not simple and that a series of "criteria hurdles" have to be overcome. The project could have foundered on any of these issues, but at the end probably the most important criterion was that in terms of strategy, the project had to go ahead: to turn away from the opportunity would be to hand the competition a market gift. Where else could a company get hold of such a huge quantity of product? It will represent, even for Shell, a substantial contributor to its earnings growth over the next half century.

# CORPORATE STRATEGY AND THE PURPOSE OF BUSINESS

It has long been recognized that the activity of planning is a primary function of senior management. Indeed it is arguable that it is the primary role of the board of directors of all firms and that they should spend most of their time considering the future direction of their company. The phrase "strategic management" is now used to describe the whole process of running a business with the the future in mind – But WHY BOTHER? There are those who would argue that since the future is so uncertain spending too much time thinking about it and in planning is actually a waste of time. It is much more comfortable to worry about today's affairs than think about what might happen in three, five, or even forty years ahead, and the opportunistic business person will invest when the idea strikes without spending too much time on a cold evaluation of the logic of the proposal.

The neatest reason for planning was proposed by Russell Ackoff, who said that its purpose was *"to secure a desired future"* for the organization – in other words, to try as far as possible to ensure that the organization will survive and will actually deliver what those involved in the business want, no matter how far into the future we are looking.

All this begs the questions: *"For whom does the firm exist?"* and *"What is a successful business?"*

Firms exist for many reasons: some reasons may be altruistic or philanthropic, but most are there because the owners see the firm as a means to an end – to self-promote, to indulge in a hobby or an interest, to become powerful, or just simply to become rich. Where companies are widely owned – where their shares are quoted on stock markets – then management and ownership are separate and the problem then arises whether the company exists to secure a desired future for the owners (i.e., the shareholders) or for the managers (who may be shareholders too, in a minor way). The so-called "shareholder theory" of the firm takes the view that all decisions must be taken with the shareholders in mind, since the business exists to satisfy them, and the interests of all other parties (especially managers, employees, customers and suppliers) are subordinate to those of the owners.

In contrast, the "stakeholder theory" assumes that all vested interests (including the owners) have to be satisfied. This may lead to a conflict of interests, most particularly in the short run where a decision which gives short-term satisfaction to one group may well cause dissatisfaction with another. For example, a significant increase in all-round pay to employees may well leave insufficient funds for paying an appropriate dividend to shareholders. Similarly, management may want higher levels of research expenditure to secure the future of the firm, whereas the owners may want short-term rewards. Indeed, in these situations the shareholder is sometimes referred to as "the residual legatee" – those who get what's left over.

These conflicts occur where there is a lack of appreciation and agreement (by any side) of what is best for the long-term survival and prosperity of the business. Unless the company exists simply to fulfill a project and is then disbanded, it is probably the norm that all parties wish to see the firm have a very long-term future. Even so, the "Anglo-Saxon tradition" (i.e., firms in the Americas and Britain) tend to take the view that shareholder satisfaction is the prime purpose, whereas the continental European and Japanese traditions are more stakeholder oriented.

# THE BIG STRATEGIC QUESTION

Business strategy concerns itself with the question:

• What do we have to do to keep our shareholders satisfied?

This leads to two further questions:

• What are the long-term aims and objectives of the business?
• How are these objectives to be realized?

One immediate difficulty lies in the words "satisfied shareholder" since in a company with wide share ownership individuals may well have differing views about what constitutes satisfaction. Generally it can be assumed that satisfied shareholders are prepared to leave their money in the business and even support it when the going gets a bit tough. This implies faith in the management, in the products or services being sold, in its financial strength and its financial performance, and in the way in which it is investing for the future. Crudely and simply, firms are viewed as "prospects" by shareholders and potential shareholders by reference to another difficult question:

• Will the company use my money wisely to create more wealth for me (in the long haul) than any other similar company?

# AIMS AND OBJECTIVES OF BUSINESS ENTERPRISES

---

**♦ A SELF-TEST AND AN ACTION ♦**

Do you know what the aims and objectives are of the company you know best? If not, either ask, if you work in a business, or get hold of the company's latest Annual Report and Accounts, which should (these days) say something about what they are trying to do!

---

# 1 Survive

Most firms are in business for the long haul and survival is really a minimum requirement. However, there is a strategic consideration in this objective, because no business has a divine right to exist. All firms are vulnerable to a greater or lesser extent to influences, both internal and external, which can cause collapse. Major factors include:

**One good reason for making a strategic investment is to minimize the threat which these factors pose.**

- Competition, which rarely gives favours;
- Economic trends (including inflation, recession, currency depreciation and high interest rates);
- Technological advances making one's own products obsolete;
- Human resource issues such as lack of suitable staff;
- Inefficiency leading to insufficient profits and cash.

One good reason for making a strategic investment is to minimize the threat which these factors pose.

# 2 Grow

Many firms see growth as a key ambition, the argument being that standing still is risky and the owners will only be satisfied if the cake gets bigger each year. Growth can be assessed in many ways, including :

- Volume of product sold (a favourite in the motorcar industry);
- Sales revenues (a dangerous measure on its own since high sales growth may lead to cashflow problems);
- Profits (before tax or net income) and earnings (i.e., net income) per share;
- Dividends paid;
- Total assets employed;
- Equity capital. This conflicts with dividend growth, since a company paying no dividend will grow its equity capital base faster than a firm paying out high dividends.

13

- Market capitalization. This is defined as the total value of the company on the stock market and only applies to quoted companies (i.e., the share price multiplied by the number of shares in issue).

Underlying all these is the notion that wealth needs to be created; not only making profit but being able to grow the value of the investment made by the owners.

## 3 Be big

Some companies want to be big, either in terms of their market capitalization or in sales terms where their market share becomes important. Other measures used are purely physical units – like the number of employees. Particular industries have their own favorite measures: airlines use passenger miles, road haulage uses ton miles, the paint industry uses pints of paint.

There are two main drawbacks to being big. First it draws unwelcome attention from groups who have legal, social or moral objections to such size. Second, being big is no guarantee of prosperity, nor even of survival. The economies of scale are often balanced by diseconomies.

## 4 Make a profit

Profit is made only when something is sold (or hired out). Failure to make a profit threatens the survival of every commercial undertaking and is therefore just as fundamental an aim as survival.

The advantage of a financial objective, like profit, is that it is usually expressed in numerical form and it is easy to compare the actual result achieved with the objective. So if a company wants a profit next year of £1 million and only achieves £900 thousand, it is plain for all to see that it has failed in its objective. When specific numbers are attached to objectives in this way, it is usual to refer to them as "goals." In other words they are specific targets to aim at. Most companies use the term "profit" in their statement of objectives. Unfortunately, on its own, profit is a meaningless statement since there is no universally agreed "legal" definition of the term; it can

14

be defined in many different ways and is subject to value judgement.

Profit measures are however useful targets to aim at, assuming consistency of definition, but they do not lend themselves to comparison – mainly because inflation distorts the value of money over time. Indeed, as we will see later, investment appraisal techniques which build in an element of inflation invariably appear more attractive. Moreover, to have as an objective "to make a profit" is too simple: $1 would meet the objective. To make an *adequate* profit is a better objective, but this leaves unanswered the question of "What is *adequate*," which is where the objective of "profitability" or "return on capital" is helpful.

## 5  Be profitable

If you put £100 into a British building society (savings and loan business in the USA) and receive interest at the end of the year of £6, the return on your investment is six percent. Similarly if you were a rich shipping magnate and spent £100 million on a pair of new cruise-liners which brought in a profit of £6 million (after tax), your return on investment would also be six percent. In both cases the equation can be called *profitability*; it is an expression of the successful use of the basic resources of the business – money and people. All businesses are the same in this respect: money is put in and used by people to obtain facilities, equipment and other resources which are used by others to produce and sell goods and services. The activities should yield a money surplus if the operation has been well run. If badly run, there is no surplus, no profit and ultimately the firm expires. To put in £100 and get £25 out each year is a very different to only getting £2 out. The more we get out the more profitable we are.

---

**DANGER – measures of profitability can mislead and deceive**

---

Possibly the most easily accessible profitability measure is that of return on equity, which shows net profit after tax (net income) as a

Profitability is often referred to as "return on capital" or "return on investment" or "return on assets." Indeed there are more than one hundred ways of measuring the concept – an enormous trap for the unwary – and even though they all measure the same concept, the precise calculation may result in a satisfactory, or unsatisfactory number, depending on the choice of numerator and denominator. Here are a few of the items used to construct the ratio, generically described as:

$$\frac{\textbf{PROFIT}}{\textbf{CAPITAL}}$$

NUMERATOR = PROFIT*
- Trading or operating profit
- Profit before interest and tax (PBIT or EBIT)
- Profit before tax (PBT or EBT)
- Net income (net profit after tax)
- Net income before extraordinary items

DENOMINATOR = CAPITAL†
- Total assets
- Total assets less current liabilities
- Equity capital (shareholders' funds)
- Equity plus long-term debt
- Equity plus all debt
- Operating assets only

\* Profit, however defined, is for one financial (i.e., 12 months) year so that an annual return is obtained.
† Capital may be taken as at the start of the financial year or at the end, or an average of both.

percentage of the shareholders' equity funds. *Fortune* magazine uses the year-end value of equity when it calculates the statistics for the *"Fortune 500"* league tables. It is a measure showing how well the company has used the shareholders' money and as such is a good overall measure of success. The average return for the largest US corporations, as measured by *Fortune,* is in the region of 10 percent to 14 percent ( and always has been). In 1994 the median was 13.7 percent, with an upper decile (i.e., company number 50 in the league) of 25.4 percent and a lower decile of 8.1 percent. The range is even greater with many firms making negative returns and a few generating returns of over 30 percent, including the Coca-Cola Corporation which turned in a remarkable 48.8 percent.

Statistics for European countries are not so comprehensively available, but it appears that the average and range of results for European firms is not too dissimilar to that of US companies.

What is an adequate return? Profit is needed for two main things:

> **An adequate profit is one which gives a level of profitability which adequately rewards the owners for the risk taken and to enable the business to grow.**

- To give to the investors as a reward for tying up their money in something more or less risky.
- To purchase assets to build the business (i.e., reinvest).

An adequate profit, therefore, is one which gives a level of profitability which adequately rewards the owners for the risk taken and to enable the business to grow.

## 6 Be efficient

Efficiency on its own is not usually regarded as the primary objective of companies, but rather as an essential ingredient with other objectives. For example, a builder may have the objective of "efficient house construction," a bank may wish to be "an efficient lender and borrower of money." Only two things need to be said about efficiency in the context of strategy. First, no company can be 100 percent efficient – there is always scope for improvement – and no strategy can succeed if the business is inefficient. Second, there is no point in being efficient if nobody is interested in the results anyway. The most efficient manufacturer of steam engines in the world has very little future.

## 7 Provide a service

Most commercial organizations which sell services, as opposed to making products, have to make sure that the services which are offered are appealing, and in demand. It is a matter for the company to decide if this should be the primary objective, or whether the provision of the service is the means to the end. This objective is often associated with not-for-profit organizations, such as charities or in the public sector, where profit is not the primary aim.

## 8 Satisfy the owners

A highly profitable company is able to give its shareholders a good return on their investment and also plough back considerable funds into the firm. This should enable it to grow faster and make even bigger profits so it can give the owners an even greater return. When this is linked to the price of the shares on a stockmarket, the "market value" of the company and the individual shareholder's wealth all rise. This leads to satisfied owners, though precisely what level of return and growth actually does satisfy a shareholder is a moot point.

## 9 Be the most respected in one's field

Many firms would consider it not just enough to be profitable and to achieve reasonable levels of growth, but will feel that to be recognized as a "good" company adds to its aims a qualitative measure which is just as desirable. It could be argued that to be the most respected is necessary for long-term financial success and include it as a supporting objective, rather than a primary aim. Even so, to be recognized as "the best", however this is defined, is a challenging objective to declare.

# LAST WORDS ON OBJECTIVES

Objectives must always be SMART:

- Specific
- Measurable
- Achievable
- Realistic
- Time-set

Whatever the objective, the end result, or the *corporate mission*, is to create and maintain a successful business. So: *What is a successful business?*

There are many answers to this question, but it is fair to say that success can be described in financial terms, for example – *to add sufficient value in the long run for the owners to be satisfied with their investment* – but also in qualitative terms, for example – *to be recognized as the best and most respected business in one's chosen field of endeavor.*

Consider this quotation:

*Success will be measured by our ability over time to fulfill our "promise" through the development of pioneer healthcare products and services to improve the quality of life for people everywhere. Simultaneously we are committed to delivering a solid return on total invested capital to our shareholders.*

*To achieve success, we have focused our energy and resources on three targets: developing and implementing a winning strategy; treating our people as our most important asset and measuring performance and reward accordingly.*

Jan Leschly, Chief Executive, SmithKline Beecham, Annual Report 1995.

◆

In business, before a strategy is chosen the facts must be gathered about the ability of the company to fight, and about the nature of the world in which it intends to operate.

◆

# Chapter 2

◆

# STRATEGIC AUDIT AND THE BUSINESS ENVIRONMENT
## How to carry out a strategic analysis

*Plans are nothing; planning is everything.*
Dwight D. Eisenhower

The term "strategy" derives from the Greek words meaning "to lead an army" and implicit in this simple statement is the notion that there is a war to be won. In business it may seem like warfare, but it is often difficult to identify the enemy and it also seems as though the war is never won – every new day brings new challenges for the company. In war, the successful leader has to gather information before deciding a strategy – information about the enemy, the terrain, the conditions that might prevail and also facts about the capabilities and capacities of one's own troops. In the same way in business, before a strategy is chosen the facts must be gathered about the ability of the company to fight, and about the nature of the world in which it intends to operate. This is the process of Strategic Analysis which is often simplistically referred to as SWOT analysis – the need to identify:

- the **S**trengths and **W**eaknesses of the organization itself
- the **O**pportunities and **T**hreats in the environment of the business.

# STRATEGIC AUDIT

The term Strategic Audit refers to the systematic and comprehensive assessment of every part of the current business – its strengths and weaknesses. The reason for analysis of a firm's strengths and weaknesses is simple: strong points have to be maintained and form the basis of many successful strategies. In contrast a weakness has to be avoided if at all possible: one must not trust a weak link and ideally it should be cured. Successful companies have learned this lesson; failures have ignored it. This is not the whole story, though. Corporate success or failure may also result from factors outside the firm's control, but there is a better chance of achieving corporate objectives if the factors over which the company has control are identified and managed. Imagine the army commander who tries to get a batallion to attack without first finding out if there are enough fit, fresh soldiers, adequately armed, clothed and fed and with the appropriate levels of support behind (and above).

It is helpful to begin with the accounting and statistical information of the company because using numbers helps to pinpoint more accurately relative strengths and weaknesses. For example, to assert that the managers are "a bunch of old fogies" is not as believable as saying that their average age is 62.5 years. Similarly to say that "our distribution costs are too high" is only credible if the statement can be proved in numbers, like £2 a mile compared to an industry average of £1.50 a mile.

To be really helpful, numbers need to be handled in a special way. It is of little use to say: "Last year the plant produced a million cans of beer," because it is impossible to form a value judgment about the volume made. It is better to compare the number with the previous year or with the competition: "Last year we produced one million cans of beer, almost 200 thousand more than the year before and more than any of our competitors." Moreover if the object of the exercise is to assess such things as efficiency and productivity, it is even better to use percentages and other ratios like cost per hour and output per employee: "Last year we produced 55 thousand cans per employee, compared with the previous year of only 50 thousand cans, a productivity increase of 10 percent."

It is only when numbers are used in this way that the manager can make valid assessments of the strength or weakness of the different areas of the business by using the data to make comparisons: to benchmark everything that is done within the business.

## Standards and benchmarks for making comparisons

There are four standards for making comparisons. They are:

- The past
- Other units in the same company
- Other organizations
- Internal targets and standards

### The benchmarked athlete

A keen athlete was determined to be good at the 1500 m race and trained long and hard to be quicker. She had four standards by which she measured her progress. First, she kept a record of the time taken every time she ran the distance and always strived to better her previous best. She also judged her performance against the best members of her club and was determined to run faster than the club record. She also had regard for the time taken at the Olympics and at the world Championships. These gave her the benchmarks for her own target, which was to be the fastest over the distance, and her training schedules were designed to eliminate the factors which were inhibiting her from attaining her goal.

The analogy is clear: benchmark against the best in the league, for this gives a measure of how much scope there is for improvement, but also identifies within an organization those parts which need most attention and those parts which are the foundation stones of future success.

# KEY AREAS TO EXAMINE

## 1 Financial resources

Two issues are of major concern in this critical area of the business: the financial strength of the firm and the extent of risk.

Financial strength centers on how much money a company has and how much it can generate from its operations or raise or borrow and how much interest it has to pay on its debts. Shortage of money seems to be a "popular" weakness these days, even in companies that are doing well by other criteria. A shortage of money may arise in a successful company if it has recently invested heavily in new equipment or has grown fast, absorbing a large quantity of working capital in the process (in inventories and accounts receivable – "debtors"). Also, if the company has aquired another firm and paid cash for it a shortage of money may well arise. The weakness in this case is that any further strategic investment may not be possible immediately, even though the firm appears successful in other respects.

A shortage of money is much more serious if it is coupled with an inability to borrow money or raise it internally, for instance by reducing working capital levels or by selling off assets no longer needed. In this case the weakness prohibits strategic investment and could easily cause corporate collapse.

Risk in this context is the question of getting involved in activities which may fail (or which may do extremely well). Risk is also affected by how much money is tied up in foreign currencies which may be subject to adverse exchange rate fluctuations. Financial risk itself usually refers to the extent a firm has borrowed money. This is referred to as "gearing" or "leverage" and is a serious weakness if the firm's trading performance is so poor that it cannot pay the interest on the debts, nor even repay the money borrowed. On the other hand, ability to borrow, or "debt capacity" is a strength.

Financial strength makes most strategic decisions possible. Financial weakness closes down a firm's options and makes only one outcome possible if not cured – closedown.

> **Financial strength makes most strategic decisions possible. Financial weakness closes down a firm's options.**

## 2 Physical resources

Companies need adequate physical facilities to keep costs down, provide for additional business and, where customers are concerned, to give a prompt and pleasant service. Old buildings and equipment are not only unattractive but also often relatively inefficient. Reliability becomes a problem and maintenance expenditure goes up. Old equipment may also be technologically out of date (especially in the computer world).

As far as the capacity of physical resources is concerned, it would seem at first that a firm operating at full capacity has a strength. It is, though, a weakness because it limits the capacity of the business to grow organically. To be unable to meet an upsurge in demand because of some physical limitation is a frustrating lost opportunity. Equally there is no point in spending huge sums on promotional activities if the equipment cannot expand output.

A further physical resource weakness is the actual location of the firm. It is clearly a weakness for a manufacturing company to be based in Germany when its major market is the USA, just as an hotel located in the middle of the Sahara may find customers scarce. To be near the source of materials, or markets, can be a great strength.

## 3 Human resources

The main questions to be answered with regard to people are:

- Have they the competences and capabilities to grow the business?
- Are certain skills missing?
- Can we obtain more quickly or do we have to grow our talent?

Human resource audit has a difficult problem to face – how do we know what is wanted unless a strategy has first been proposed? On the other hand, a strategy can only be proposed if we know what our human resource strengths are now. The way out of the dilemma is that the human resource audit should be capable of answering the question: "If we do pursue a certain strategy, have we the people to see it through – *without wrecking our core business at the same time?*"

## 4 Products and services

A well-developed range of products or services is one of a company's greatest strengths. Conversely, a firm with weak products seems to struggle to keep afloat. Among the key factors to examine are:

- Price levels
- Share of the market
- Perception of the product or service by customers
- "Appeal."

Also of critical importance is the stage in the product's life cycle:

- Is it growing in demand?
- At a mature stage?
- Likely to decline in the near future?

This last stage is a difficult notion to measure. Even so, if all one's products start to decline at the same time trouble is not far away. The so-called Boston Box (Figure 2.1) is a useful way of looking at the nature of the products in a company's portfolio. Developed by the Boston Consulting Group four basic characteristics can be identified:

- **Stars** are fast-growing products and, because of the company's high market share, are likely to do well in the future. However at this stage the product absorbs money (for promotion and development costs, for instance).

- **Cash cows** are products that have passed through the high-growth stage, are now mature and need no further investment. They "make money."

26

- The **Problem** products could do well if the growth continues, but the investment required is greater than that for the **Stars**. If the low market share can be turned into a higher share, then there is a chance of success. There is a chance that they will turn into **Dogs**.

  **Stars cash cows problems dogs . . . .**

- **Dogs** are products to be rid of. Their volume is too low fully to utilize the resources assigned to them and they are probably not contributing much to the profits of the company.

**Figure 2.1**

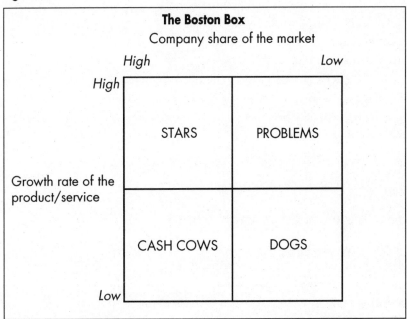

A final question in the audit of one's product/service range is: What is being developed by us which will be tomorrow's stars? If there is nothing in the pipeline, a strategic investment decision may take the form of rectifying this particular omission.

## The value chain

Value chain analysis was developed by Michael Porter as a way of identifying the elements of a business that contributed to (or

THE STRATEGIC INVESTMENT DECISION

detracted from) its competitive advantage – having products or services which are different from the rest of the market and which secure the firm's position. The primary activities of business are:

- Inbound logistics
- Operations
- Outbound logistics
- Marketing and sales
- Services

These are supported by other activities, "support activities," namely procurement, technology development, human resource management, and infrastructure.

> **"Does the activity give us any competitive advantage?"**

Each has to be evaluated to establish its contribution to the business and, indeed, benchmarking in each activity can give strong indicators of relative value. In all, the questions must always be asked: "Does the activity give us any competitive advantage? Do we need to boost the activity, or get rid of it, or do it in a different way?"

## Last word on the strategic audit

Unless this activity is carried out, then strategic decisions run the risk of failing to turn out as you expect. Some element in your organization will not be able to meet the needs of the strategy. It has to be thorough, regular, systematic, and appropriately measured and benchmarked.

# ASSESSING OPPORTUNITIES AND THREATS

All companies are affected by events outside their control and a firm's survival and success depends on how skilfully its managers handle these external influences. A company that does no planning – has no strategy – is trusting that the future will stay much the same as today. In contrast a firm that tries to anticipate how its environment is changing stands a much better chance of prospering. The history of business on both sides of the Atlantic over the last twenty years has many tales of firms going under because they were unable to cope with shifts in their business world. In the USA, deregulation of air transport led to the demise of several well-known carriers. In the UK, Laker Airways failed in large measure because of external forces. Also in the UK, government regulations forced regional television companies to reapply for licenses to broadcast and as a result Thames Television, among others, found itself deprived of its license and, as a result, the bulk of its revenues (from advertising).

In contrast, some firms have emerged which have taken the place of yesterday's star players or which are doing things that did not happen a while ago. They have recognized the changing world and have created businesses that "fit" the new order:

- Bodyshop has captured a changing attitude to the way people view the environment.
- Microsoft has pioneered the phenomenal growth of home computer applications.

For existing companies there would be no problem if the business environment in which the firm was operating was stable and never changed. Unfortunately it does change and just to make life interesting the rate of change is not consistent.

To illustrate this idea, consider weather forecasting. Most people live in climates which show a variation over the year. It is known that winter will turn to summer; it is known that sun will be followed by rain and by snow (for some of us), and that the temperature will rise and fall. But what is not known is :

- When will the weather change?
- What will it change to?
- Will it change completely (if global warming happens)?

An alternative approach is to ask:

- How long will the present weather last?
- When it does change, will it be for better or worse?

Climate is one of the most unpredictable environments, although fortunately the range of possible types of weather that any one place at any one time can experience is fairly limited. Moreover, there is an annual cycle which can safely be predicted a long time ahead.

Future events are, therefore, of two types: the predictable (the weather is unlikely to be freezing in London in July; General Motors is unlikely to go bust); and the unpredictable (the precise temperature in London in July; General Motors' precise profit or loss).

Shell can reasonably predict that there will be a demand for natural gas well into the twenty-first century. But what price will they be able to sell it for? How do they know that there will not be another source of cheap heating by 2040 AD?

In this case *the planning horizon* is over fifty years and has to be so given the nature of the oil industry. Its long-term opportunity is that that the gas will be in demand for fifty years and the threat that there will be cheaper energy sources before then.

For a very small business – the local grocery store, for instance – the long-term future may have little relevance. The owner's planning horizon will be a year or two at the most. Changes that are likely to affect it can be accommodated without too much strategic thinking. The changes are incremental and adaptability is the key to success – taking on board new ideas and new products as they arise.

It would appear that with larger companies it takes longer and longer to change their set-up to meet changes in the environment. A small boat can change direction quickly, but it takes a giant supertanker many miles and much time to change course. Many new developments can take over ten years from the initial recognition that something needs to be done, through to full production. Aircraft, power stations, Eurotunnel and the Troll Gasfield are all good examples – simply because they are so complicated and expensive to design, develop, and build. The questions which need to be considered regarding the environment are:

- What aspects of the environment have to be taken into account in planning and what can safely be ignored?

- Is there any way of anticipating what is going to happen?
- How far ahead should companies try to estimate what is going to happen?
- How can a company minimize the threats from the environment that lie ahead and take advantage of the opportunities which may exist?

# ASPECTS OF THE BUSINESS ENVIRONMENT

What aspects of the business environment (the outside world) have to be taken into account? Consider this case.

There was once a small town bookstore. It was busy and profitable and the owners always had the problem that they could not carry in stock or on the shelves all the books, cards, journals, and stationery lines for which there appeared to be a continuing demand. One day the opportunity arose to acquire the premises next door. The price seemed right, but the family debate centered around the fundamental question, "Will the demand for the lines we sell be enough to compensate for the additional investment and operating costs we will incur?" One member of the family was convinced that sales turnover would grow substantially, but another view – held by the accountant member of the family – was not so positive. She said: "I can think of at least half a dozen reasons why demand could stop growing." Among the reasons given were:

- Inflation might push prices so high that people would spend less on books.
- There might be a downturn in economic activity in the area, and less spending money about as a result.
- A competitor in the next street might well begin to sell more aggressively.
- There may be a trend away from reading as cable and satellite TV and multimedia computers grow in popularity.
- The local government elections were coming up soon and one of the political parties appeared keen to redevelop the whole area in which the shop was located.

- The population might decline, if the birth rate slows or if people move away to more attractive regions.

All these reasons reflect aspects of the bookstore's environment which could affect it and the possibilities can be grouped into several different types of environment. This helps make analysis more effective.

The first and second reasons deal with money matters and could be described as the "economic" environment. The third is the "competitive" environment. The fourth is partly reflecting trends in the "social" environment of the business, but is also identifying the changes in its "technological" world. The "political" environment of the business needed to be closely monitored. The last reason was "demographic," although a wider category might be termed the "natural" environment since we could also include phenomena such as climatic change and "forces of nature."

These six different environments are a convenient way of classifying the world around the organization, and each needs a closer look.

## 1 The economic environment

Probably no organization can avoid being affected by the economic environment. Again the state of the economy is continuously changing and the company that succceeds is the one that identifies rising and falling trends fastest and takes action soonest, or which has sufficient flexibility to adapt to the new economic situation. The economic environment has many aspects and the main ones that affect companies are the prosperity of the market, inflation, exchange rates, and interest rates.

### The prosperity of the market

Using the word "market" in the widest sense to mean all the possible customers for the company's goods and services, it is not hard to see that if customers are not feeling well off (absence of the so-called "feel-good factor") they are not likely to spend as much. Some firms are more sensitive to the ups and downs of the economy than others. Firms in the motor trade, whether manufacturers or dealers, are very vulnerable because the sale of new cars falls off rapidly when times are not so good. The problem for motor dealers especially is that they buy from the manufacturers in anticipation of being able to sell. The manufacturers produce in anticipation of being able to sell to dealers. If the customers do not come into the showrooms and buy, the dealer is left with a heap of new cars, little

> **If you know that boom times lay ahead your decision would be easier, but if you think it may not be so good what action do you take?**

money in the bank, and the problem of paying next month's wages. The manufacturer finds that orders are drying up and has to cut production, operate shorter shifts and order less (or nothing) from component suppliers.

In terms of the strategic decision, if you knew that boom times lay ahead your decision would be easier, but if you think it may not be so good what action do you take?

### Inflation

Inflation is known to everyone as increases in the price we have to pay for goods in the shops. All companies, in inflationary times, find that they have to pay out more for the goods and services that they are using than they did previously. Raw material costs rise, wages rise, fuel and power costs more, and so on. For a time firms can offset these rises by increasing the prices of their own products or services to compensate. But eventually resistance will be encountered and a fall in demand results.

Strategically, an investment proposition always "looks" better if future profits are given an inflation factor. This is dangerous and misleading, as we will see.

### Exchange rates

Companies involved in buying from other countries or which sell into other countries, as well as those which are set up in more than one separate economic state, are particularly concerned about the way exchange rates fluctuate, because a great deal of money can be lost if the wrong currency is being held at the wrong time. Moreover, buying goods from overseas at the wrong time can cost a

Siemens' decision to build a factory in the UK partly reflects the very favorable Sterling/Deutsche mark exchange rate as far as Germany is concerned. The UK appeared "cheap." However Siemens must also have a view that, since a high percentage of output will be exported from UK, exchange rate fluctuations were, on balance, likely to enhance earnings rather than become an invisible "discount."

great deal of profit, just as selling into an overseas market at the wrong time can also bring in less income. Even simply owning assets in another country can have an adverse impact on the company's results if the currency of the overseas country depreciates.

**The strategic decision needs to be aware of the exchange rate risk when international investment is considered.**

The strategic decision needs to be aware of the exchange rate risk when international investment is considered.

### Interest rates

Interest is the cost of borrowing as well as the reward for lending, and these days there are very few companies that manage without having to borrow money at one time or another. There are many advantages to borrowing. (There are risks too as we mentioned on gearing), on page 24 but the timing of the borrowing can be critical. For instance, a company decided to build a new factory with a capital investment cost of £2 million. The firm had the opportunity to borrow at a fixed rate of 10 percent per annum for ten years (£200,000 of interest a year off the profits), but the firm was slow to take a decision and six months later the money could only be borrowed at 12 percent (£240,000 a year interest). The extra £40,000 represents a drop of no less than 2 percent on the simple return on the investment.

The strategic decision should not be taken *per se* on whether the source of capital is debt rather than equity. Nevertheless, if interest costs have to be taken into account then the company must be conscious of the additional financial risk being taken on.

## 2 Competition

Possibly the best-known element in the environment of the firm is the competition. "Know your enemy" applies in business just as much as in warfare. The first problem for a company is to define exactly who the competition is. For example, some years ago in the UK, tea was promoted as "the best drink of the day," which gives rise to the obvious question: "By comparison with what?" A moment's thought suggests some interesting competitors for tea – coffee being the most obvious, but what about beer, lemonade, cola, milk, scotch, or even plain water?

It is the job of the marketing function in the company to study the market in which the product or service competes to establish not just what are the competitors but which are the relevant competitors – those which are competing in your segments of the market. Rolls Royce is not competing with Honda.

It is not particularly difficult to find out something about one's competitors and their products and services: it is much more difficult to find out about those firms who will be competing against you in the future. The European and American motor manufacturers were aware of the competition that existed amongst themselves, but they failed to appreciate the threat that would emerge from the Japanese car makers – almost too late in some cases.

The competitive strategy has to recognize that firms do not stand still and that the marketplace is constantly being changed by companies doing something new. A "me too" strategy – being a follower – sometimes pays off, but where technological innovation captures the cream of a market, being the first in the field is most likely to produce the best dividend. But to be first, most investment has to be made.

## 3 Social

The social environment of a company can change as much as any other. Sometimes the changes are less obvious with social trends often going unnoticed for some time. Consider these social trends: anti-smoking; the Green issue; the increase in holidays abroad; vegetarianism and eating out. They are all long-term trends which have favored some organizations, but greatly harmed others. Some social trends come and go fast – rollerblading is a recent new craze and some are making big profits from it. (If you are not in the business now it is probably too late.) Consider also the fashion business, and entertainment and leisure; the trends are rapidly up and just as fast down.

As far as a firm's strategy is concerned, it must be prepared to change track completely if its social climate is deteriorating. Again this involves significant investment decisions – and very brave ones, too. If fads and fashions are the firm's business it must be prepared to take the risks of leadership and not be "a dedicated follower of fashion."

## 4 Technological environment

Is there much demand these days for slide rules, gas lights or steam engines? Slide rules have been replaced by calculators, gas is used for heating and cooking only, and steam engines are only found as museum pieces or in odd corners of the world which cannot afford newer forms of locomotion. These are all examples of products which are no longer in use because something better has come along to do the job.

The changes in the technological environment (using the word in the widest possible sense) that have been seen over the last fifty years have been immense, particularly in such areas as pharmaceuticals, chemicals, and electronics. Space-age technology, as it is termed, is changing so fast that what was new just a few months ago will have been superseded by something even better – or in some cases, something making the old-style product obsolete. The calculator has made the slide rule redundant, and the oldest calculators now look "old-fashioned."

Technological change is important in three ways:

- First, there is the problem that competitors may achieve a technological development which may bite into your own market share. What is worse is an entirely new form of opposition from a different type of competitor. For example, the electrically powered motorcar is being developed by the motor industry but also by others, notably battery makers.

- Second, companies have to be aware of general technological advances in the broad area which they can build into their own products.

- Third, all firms use equipment of one kind or another, even if it is merely the usual kind of office equipment – phones, computers, photocopiers and printers. Technology is uprating and updating all the equipment used by companies at a very fast rate and there is no doubt that for many firms one of the most difficult decisions is when to replace out-of-date, but perfectly efficient, equipment.

---

### ◆ POINT TO PONDER ◆

At home, unless it is brand new, much of the equipment in the kitchen – or for leisure, like the television – may be a few years old. It is therefore out of date. Would you have a policy to keep everything until it stopped working or automatically to trade it in every four years, say, for the latest version? Or would you pass the item on to a relative after five or six years and buy a new one?

---

In strategic terms, companies must keep their products and services as modern as possible and must also ensure that their "means of production" – the technologies they use to make, build or provide the service – are the most efficient and cost effective available. However, strategically, the company that makes the technological leap forward is going to have the best chance of coming out "top." Microsoft has not been a follower of technological change, it has been the leader. In all such cases the investment decisions are based on the view that it is better to change the marketplace than try to fight over an existing, mature market: much more risky (there are thousands of dud inventions around), but enormous rewards for success.

## 5 Political and legal environment

All companies have to exist within the political and legal system wherever they operate. Domestically, politics can be national or local, and even at international level, when considering for example, the European Union or the North Atlantic Free Trade Area (NAFTA). All levels can have a significant impact on the life and well being of the firm. If the political party in power never changed or if policies never changed, then life would be much simpler. But it is the way of political life that there is change from time to time and if it changes too frequently it is very difficult to decide what actions to take. Some political parties are prepared to spend more money, others are not. Some have free trade policies and encourage organizations to set up in different countries, or help with exporting and allow unrestricted importing. Other parties discourage such activities.

As far as a company is concerned which operates across national frontiers, the worst type of country to deal with is one with political instability; the next group to come to power may not view one favorably.

---

### ♦ POINT TO PONDER ♦

There are those who believe that China will be a major international economic force in the twenty-first century and that a great deal of money can be made there. Some argue that, strategically, now is the time to get involved in the country and actually invest – a "pre-emptive strike" to keep out the competition. However, others recognize that China's political future is uncertain and that there is a chance of losing money as well as making it. How do you view it? Would you invest?

---

The political environment is not only important in relation to trade and business but also in many other respects. Some governments delight in creating laws that increase the number of forms which have to be completed. Others, at all levels, have an attitude of *laissez-faire*, letting companies get on with it with the minimum of interference. In contrast, there are those that pass many laws of a restrictive nature, effectively making it illegal to do certain things. All companies have to live within an active political environment and have to be aware that what they do could be the object of some political action.

## 6 Natural

For some companies the forces of nature are the most important aspects of the environment which need to be watched. The weather is of critical importance to farmers and the food and drink industries, though prediction can, as we have seen, be difficult. But a firm can plan to minimize the risks from adverse situations. If you sell icecream, you should be able to meet demand if there is a scorching summer, but have enough storage capacity to keep your products if summer turns out cold and wet.

Demographic changes can also affect a firm's market and these should be closely monitored – if you sell babyclothes in a town with a declining birthrate your strategy should be "Get out of town."

# ANTICIPATING WHAT MIGHT HAPPEN

Is there any way of anticipating what might happen? In short, the answer is "no." However, there has to be an attempt and several specific aids are available to try to reduce the uncertainty about the future.

**Futurology** is the term applied to the technique of trying to assess what the environment might look like many years ahead, assuming current trends continue. These produce scenarios – "pictures" of what the world might look like.

The **Delphi technique** relies on expert opinion to assess the likelihood of certain situations emerging at some specific date in the future. For example, if you want to know how soon electrically powered motorcars will be commonplace, ask as many experts as you can find. There may (hopefully) be a concensus answer, which should prove a fairly reliable guide – but repeat the exercise regularly to refine the forecast.

**Economic models** are a popular means of forecasting economic factors one or two years ahead, by putting a considerable amount of historic data into a computer and then making some assumptions about the way an economy "behaves" and about the cause-

and-effect relationships that occur within an economy. However, their limitation is often that the relationships are not as directly obvious as suggested and there is an assumption about central government economic policy, as well as the economic state of other major trading countries. Finally, they assume that people are rational all the time when it comes to economic affairs, which is probably true some of the time.

**Market forecasts** are used in a company to assess likely demand for the firm's products and services, taking into consideration all the external evidence collected by the techniques discussed above. The statistical methods used can be complex, but they can and do provide better forecasts than if the "same as last year plus a bit" technique is used.

# ESTIMATING AHEAD

How far ahead should companies try to estimate what is going to happen? The answer depends on the problem. If you want to have a barbecue today you do not need tomorrow's weather forecast, you need today's. What is needed is to be able to have enough time to be able to plan and prepare yourself to cope with some future event which, if it happens, will affect your business for better or worse. Igor Ansoff, the eminent writer on corporate strategy, has spoken about picking up weak signals from the environment – just as radar can give a defending army more time to prepare for an attack by enemy missiles. Shell's Troll gas field was first explored in the 1970s when the Cold War and the "Oil Crisis" forced western oil and gas firms to explore nearer home in friendlier political, but more hostile natural, environments. The signals were that long-term supplies could not be guaranteed from traditional sources (such as the Middle East and the former Soviet Union) and the lead time (as has proved to be the case with Troll) is very long. As was suggested on page 30, the firm's planning horizon depends on how long it takes to develop the strategy, which in turn depends on one's view about the long-term future.

40

# MINIMIZE THE THREATS, MAXIMIZE THE OPPORTUNITIES

How far can a company minimize the threats and maximize the opportunities which may present themselves? In an ideal world, a company would know well in advance what environmental issues were about to occur which were going to be detrimental to it and which changes would be of benefit. How often have you heard it said: "If only I'd known that at the time, I would have done something different?" Such is the benefit of twenty-twenty hindsight.

## Scenario planning and alternative strategies

In reality, companies have to steer a course which avoids the threats which they perceive as likely to occur, yet a course which will lead to achieving the corporate goals. As a ship at sea will steer a course which avoids storms, rocks, adverse currents and pirates, so a company will set a course that minimizes the chance of disaster. The course is the Strategy, but the fear is often present that the decision is wrong. Sometimes there may be no clear and obvious answer to the riddle of the future. Future A may be very rosy indeed, but future B may be truly awful. Consider these scenarios.

# A COMMERCIAL DILEMMA

Your company is the only one in the region which buys and sells a commodity for which the market demand is more or less stable – a fall in price is unlikely to lead to an increase in sales, though a significant price hike would drive some customers away. The commodity is bulky, expensive to buy and very expensive to store.

- You hear that supplies of the commodity *may* be adversely affected next year because the country which supplies it *may* go through a political crisis. Your strategy if you knew *for sure* that the price would rise would be to get hold of the right kind of

41

storage space and buy as much of the commodity as you could lay your hands on, getting hold of as much money as you possibly could to pay for it.

- You also hear that there is a possibility of another country in the region selling the same product on the open market at considerably lower prices, but a country completely new in the market and with a very poor infrastructure. If you knew *for sure* that this will happen, your strategy is to go there and fix a contract to supply you at the lower prices.

If either of these scenarios is equally possible – in other words the probability of either event occuring is the same – what would you do?

- If you expand your facilities and buy ahead from your existing supplier, you will be cross (and be worse off) if there is no interruption of supply, and even more depressed if the other country does sell the commodity more cheaply.
- If you decide that the other country will supply and you go ahead and change your supplier, you may lose out because the cheaper option may prove unreliable, the price may go up, and the quality may be inferior. Your old supplier may be reluctant to take you on again.

Clearly there are compromises to be made. With such an uncertain future, the scenario approach forces management to think "What if?" and choose a strategy which minimizes the "downside risk" (in this case the interrupted supply, with the enormous cost) but maximizes the "upside potential" (the chance of much cheaper supplies).

Environmental change which can be seen a long way off can be built into the company's strategy, but sudden change demands that management must be decisive enough to recognize that existing strategies no longer hold good. A new strategy is needed. Something must be done about it rather than assuming it will "go away."

♦

"Construct realistic strategies that don't require rocket science."

Jack Smith,
President and CEO,
General Motors

♦

# Chapter 3

◆

# THE PLANNING GAP AND STRATEGIC DECISIONS

The Strategic Decision, as we have seen, is in fact a set of inter-related decisions, each one following from another and the fundamental purpose of the strategy itself is to ensure as far as possible that the aims and objectives of the company are achieved. In this chapter we shall explore some of the options that are, theoretically at any rate, available to management in their search for the ideal way forward – bearing in mind the organization's competencies and capabilities on the one hand and the environment in which the business operates on the other.

# WHAT IS STRATEGY?

It is easy to see what strategy means if the context is war or even a journey – it is the way in which the basic aim will be achieved. In the case of war it is to defeat the enemy in the quickest, least costly method. To embark on a journey it is usual to have a clear idea of one's destination before setting out. The strategy is the route and the method of transport. In business we have already highlighted some strategic problems: the Hotstuff Spice Works (Chapter

> **To embark on a journey it is usual to have a clear idea of one's destination before setting out. The strategy is the route and the method of transport.**

1) had several possible strategic options. A simpler strategic problem would be the case of a small firm finding that the rent it paid was about to be doubled. The obvious action is to try to cut other costs – even reduce staff or their pay – or tinker with the way of running the firm. These are hardly strategic actions, although they are important. Instead, to extend the range of products being made and sold, or expand the sales force to attack a new market or buy up another firm in the same line of business – this is strategy.

# STEPS IN CHOOSING STRATEGIES

## 1 Establish the present position

It may seem obvious, but you do not choose to visit New York tomorrow if today you are in the middle of the Sahara in Africa. Similarly, a company would not try to double its sales of a particular product if it already held 70 percent of the market. Nor would it make sense for it to try to sell throughout North America when it was only selling its products in London, England today. Unless the firms knew where they stood now, such actions would actually result in a great deal of wasted money and frustration.

## 2 Decide on the objectives

Again it seems obvious that there must be a clear, unambiguous statement of where the firm wants to get to, but one factor needs adding: When do we want to get there?

Corporate objectives were discussed in Chapter 1 and in summary these two steps can be described in this way:

> *"Our primary objective is to achieve a profit of £42 million in four years time. Currently our profits are £20 million – the difference to be made up by selecting some suitable strategy."*

This concept can easily be portrayed graphically. See Figure 3.1.

**Figure 3.1**

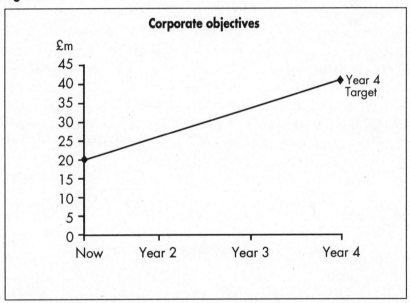

The line connecting the current year's profit with the target figure in four years' time is important only because the steepness of the slope indicates the size of the problem to be tackled – *the strategic challenge*. A company with zero or negative profits will want a dramatically steep slope since it will be in what is termed a "turnaround situation," whereas the company making a good return on investment may only wish to grow at a more modest pace.

## 3 What happens if there is a no-change strategy?

What happens to cars if they are never serviced? What happens to products which remain unchanged? What happens to companies which never recruit new blood? There are those who regard "do nothing different" as a strategy in itself, and it is fair to say that there may be times when doing nothing may be the best course of action. "Don't rock the boat" can only be justified as a strategy if it is absolutely certain that you will reach your goal traveling the way you are.

**"Don't rock the boat" can only be justified as a strategy if it is absolutely certain that you will reach your goal by traveling the way you are.**

However, it is impossible to be certain that one's objective will be reached, especially in the long term. On the other hand it is a fairly safe bet that if no changes are made to the way the company carries on its business, sooner or later it will lose its prominent position and become another "lame duck." There are thousands of examples of organizations that failed to change their ways, move with the times, refused to make changes and innovate and adapt. We can all quote large organizations which have suffered in this way (from the monarchy in France at the end of the eighteenth century through to the problems which beset IBM or the British motorcar industry some

**Figure 3.2**

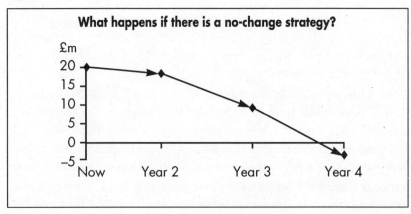

years ago). It must be remembered that small firms, too, can easily adopt a "do nothing" attitude and most people will have seen or experienced the phenomenon in action – restaurants and fashion boutiques being the most obvious. Again the idea can be displayed on a graph (see Figure 3.2).

There are dozens of reasons for this kind of pattern, but in a nutshell either its internal operations have become inefficient, or some environmental threat has become a reality. In fact, if you do nothing, your strengths evaporate, your weaknesses grow, the threats materialize, and you cannot even perceive any opportunities.

**In fact, if you do nothing, your strengths evaporate, your weaknesses grow, the threats materialize, and you cannot even perceive any opportunities.**

As far as strategy is concerned, the "do nothing new" line has to be calculated using information from the internal appraisal and the environmental evaluation. Simply, there has to be a forecast of what will happen if the present trends continue – and often the burden of responsibility for this falls to the sales or marketing functions to estimate demand under certain price parameters, having regard to the external influences. Cost trends and the impact on cash flow need also to be assessed.

There is little point in advertising or promoting heavily a product which is likely to sell well in any case. Nor is there any point in spending time and money redesigning another product's packaging if it is clearly at the end of its life cycle. Forecasts assume that nothing is done to meet the threats and opportunities coming from the environment and sooner or later there will be a downward trend. It is worth noting that the technique of long-range planning simply extrapolated from current and historical data and decisions about the future conduct of the business were taken on the basis of the "evidence" thus presented.

It is a simple matter to superimpose the "do nothing different" line on to the "where we want to be" line (see Figure 3.3).

Three things have to be noted about Figure 3.3. First, each company's chart will be different, depending on where it is at the present time and how fast its decline is projected.

Second, the two lines start together at first and often may con-

**Figure 3.3**

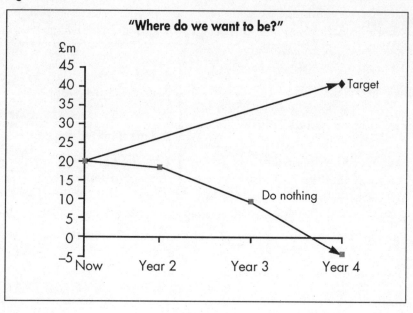

tinue closely for a year or two. It would be a lucky firm to be able to say with confidence that within four or five years nothing will happen to blow the firm off course.

The third point is that the gap between the two lines gradually widens, and the size of the gap – the *Planning Gap* – is of vital interest to the planner. It simply shows the size of the strategic challenge. In Figure 3.3 the firm wants £42 million, but if it carries on its present path it will earn a loss of £3 million. The gap is not £22 million, but £45 million and this represents new business that needs to be found.

Having identified the size of the gap, the problem is now the very difficult one of choosing suitable strategies that will fill it. Before that can be done it is worth listing the main constraints which are likely to prevent you from doing what you want.

> **Having identified the size of the gap, the problem is now the very difficult one of choosing suitable strategies that will fill it.**

## 4 What cannot be done

A detailed, complete list of things a company cannot do is endless. Instead a "top twenty" list of constraints should be constructed, some of which are the result of internal decisions, and others which are imposed upon the firm by outside agencies.

> **A threat is something in the future, a constraint is here and now.**

Internally generated constraints are previously taken decisions about what the company will not do. They emanate often from the personal values and beliefs of those senior managers who have the power within the firm. They may result in the suboptimal use of resources and force the company to accept lower returns on investment than usual – for example, the company which refuses to trade with another country, even though there are strong economic advantages in doing so, or a firm that locates in a beautiful part of the world, miles from its customers or sources of supply of people and materials, simply because the chief executive has painting as a hobby.

There are many reasons for these internally generated "laws" – religion, politics, ethics, and just plain bigotry are among the commonest. They are different to weaknesses in that there is nothing to be cured; they are constraints that have to be lived with.

Externally generated constraints include laws preventing certain types of behavior and which dictate the standards under which trade may be continued – construction industry regulations; food hygiene laws, and edicts on permissible flavors in foods; regulations governing the loading of 'planes and trucks, and so on. They are all there to protect the customer against the unscrupulous, but may also at times simply be a hindrance to making a "decent" profit. The difference between external threats and external constraints should be noted. A threat is something in the future, a constraint is here and now.

## 5 How to fill the gap?

On the face of it there is not much difference between this question and the question all firms have always asked, namely: How do we make more money? But it is a stronger question to ask: What business activities will generate a satisfactory return to our share-holders in the long run?

The search for a strategy can be undertaken in a variety of ways and a suitable starting-point is to assess the extent to which the present business can be improved.

### (i) Improvement strategies

If a company is operating with a market share of 70 percent and generating a return on investment of 35 percent, it is hardly likely that trying to grow the market share *and* maintain profitability at the same time will be possible – the scope for improvement within the existing framework is very limited. On the other hand, a firm with a low market share has considerable scope for growth without going beyond its known market. This is only worth attempting if the market is actually growing – there is little point in devoting effort to capturing more of a declining market.

A totally different problem exists for the firm that is trading unprofitably and a glance at the financial pages of the daily papers will provide evidence of companies in this category. Here the issue is, first: How do we stay alive? Current strategic thinking should be focussed on the concept of the *"turnaround strategy."* Turnaround means getting hold of an ailing business and hauling it back into reasonable levels of profit. Firms which have achieved a turnaround recently include IBM, General Motors, British Petroleum, and Royal Insurance. Companies still in the process of "going through the pain" include Trafalgar House (owners of the Cunard shipping line, and John Brown Engineering), Laura Ashley, and other companies currently making considerable losses, for example, Sony (with a loss in 1994 of $2.953 bn) and Nissan (with a loss of $1.672 bn).

How to achieve turnaround?

- Examine every item in the value chain and get rid of the marginal contributors.

- Ask: "Does it make sense to do this, or should we get others to do it for us?" This implies subcontracting and hiving off noncore activities.

- Cut out layers of management that add no value, "delayering," and restructure to reduce nonproductive activities.

- Sell off assets and even sub-business units which are marginally used.

- Cut working capital and, if necessary, defer capital expenditure.

- Get others to carry inventory for you; adopt a policy of "just-in-time."

- Restructure corporate debt (to get the banks off your back).

- Get more funds in from the shareholders – they will have to be convinced of your ability to achieve the turnaround.

- Cut dividends if possible. This is regarded as dangerous as it may adversely affect the share price. However the contra-argument is that maintaining a dividend in the face of poor results might be seen as weak management – and the shares will fall anyway.

- Focus on the core business activities for which the company will depend in the future.

- Focus on what the customer wants and make sure it is supplied – in time.

This is not an exhaustive list, but serves to illustrate the point that if a company is in difficulties, its scope for strategic action – its choice of strategies – is severely limited until it can raise its profitability and hence provide adequate cash for growth strategies.

> **If a company is in difficulties, its scope for strategic action is severely limited until it can raise its profitability and hence provide adequate cash for growth strategies.**

### (ii) Expansion strategies

Strategies that are based on improvement alone – while necessary – all suffer from the same disadvantage, namely that they are operating within the existing marketplace with a range of products and services that already exist. Consequently, they still suffer from the problem that sooner or later their markets will change, their products will lose appeal and competitive forces will erode market share. Improvement and turnaround alone merely postpone the decline illustrated by the "do nothing new" line. It has rightly been said: "We've restructured and delayered and become lean and mean. What do we do now?"

Expansion strategies are popular because they are relatively easy to introduce and have the effect of keeping everyone busy.

Strictly, expansion means expanding one of two basic business variables: either the range of products or services being offered for sale within the existing market, or selling the existing range of products in different markets. Expansion is not putting new products into new markets – that strategic move is usually termed *diversification*, which is examined more closely later.

**Product/service range expansion:** Some companies prefer to expand by adding to the list of products or services that they are selling rather than to expand the territory in which they operate. The underlying idea is that by offering customers a wider range of products there is a better chance of them buying from you rather than from the competition. Good examples are to be found in the food industry where the list of products offered by a single producer grows and grows – frozen food lines, especially ready-prepared complete meals. The motorcar manufacturers also continually widen the range of vehicles on offer – often by the means of "variation on a theme," a wide range of choice developed from a few basic models.

The advantage of product range expansion is that the additional item can easily be included in the list. The sales force need no special training; no separate distribution channels are needed; no change is needed to support systems; and indeed the extra product can often be produced on existing equipment. The chance of success should be high because the market is known and market research should have given some clues as to the likely appeal of the new item.

Unfortunately, new products can be very expensive to develop. If the company decides to innovate, as a strategic decision, it must recognize that considerable investment will be needed to get the product to market. Microsoft's "Windows 95" took huge financial resources, as well as a great deal of effort, over a long period of time before it was launched. With products where health factors are involved (pharmaceuticals and drugs especially), or in high-tech industries (aerospace and information technology), the lead times can be many years ahead. Not all additions to the product range involve investment – a retailer may be able to add to the goods on the shelf merely by ordering them from the supplier.

Where there is a significant outlay in getting a new product to market, the product's sales have to be sufficient to justify the effort, as we will see when the criteria for judging the viability of the proposal is discussed.

There is, however, no guarantee that the new line will thrive and prosper. In fact the failure rate of new products is very high – in the pharmaceutical world only one in several hundred starters actually end up as moneymakers. In general there is greater than even chance of failure, than of success.

**Market expansion:** Market expansion means the process of extending the area in which the business operates, so that more potential customers are aware of the products or services being provided.

---

#### ♦ POINT TO PONDER ♦

New products and new services are being offered to us every day of the week, often via television or advertised in the newspaper or simply being promoted on the supermarket shelves. Have you ever purchased something novel and been disillusioned, later to find it withdrawn from sale? Why did the company get it wrong?

Think of the classic failures: Ford's Edsel; a number of computer companies in recent years; the Boots Company's drug "Manuplax," withdrawn after massive research and development expenditure.

---

The most obvious examples are the chain stores – a retailer with a number of very similar shops in every city and town across a county or state. McDonald's is one of the most universally recognized, as is Kentucky Fried Chicken, where the "product" or service has been successfully implanted in many countries around the world. Inside these restaurants the same standards apply, the same products are on offer and the same style applies. The market spread has not taken place accidentally, nor simultaneously; it is the result of a deliberate strategic decision by the firm to seek growth by this method. Some firms adopting this approach favor direct investment themselves – buying the premises and paying themselves for fitting out. Most banks expand this way.

The alternative is franchising, where the franchisee carries much of the burden of investment and the risk – the owner of the brand simply selling a license to operate. The choice may be dictated by custom and practice, or by the brand owner's availability of funds. The calculation as to the viability of the project is fundamentally the same, but for the owner of the "name" different capital costs and different margins will produce different levels of attractiveness – but these have to weighed against risk.

Very often companies cannot operate at full efficiency unless they are covering a whole region or country. It is not effective to advertise your services on television if half the audience cannot buy them. This strategy is attractive for several reasons:

- It is easy to implement. A project team is needed which will go into the market and set it up, assuming that there is adequately trained management available to "open up shop" and begin selling.

- The products or services can easily be transferred into the new market and the additional volume going through the system is a strong lever for better terms from suppliers.

- Theoretically, the possibility of something going wrong is not very high because the products or services being offered are known to be acceptable – they have a track record in one market. Unfortunately, this can sometimes backfire on a firm: just because the market in the UK likes it does not guarantee its success in France. Marks & Spencer's first foray into France cost the firm dear – the French shoppers' expectations do differ from the British. In the same way, Disney's experience with Eurodisney – very disappointing levels of attendance in the early years – shows that even the most sophisticated evaluation process is not foolproof.

Another problem with geographic expansion is that the further away from home base you go, the more difficult it is to keep things under control. British firms trying to grow into the US market have often found that remote control is difficult and a disproportionate amount of managerial effort and cost (totally unpredicted in the costings) results. The London-based Midland Bank had a near disastrous experience after taking over the Californian Crocker Bank in the 1980s.

Another form of market expansion occurs not geographically – which requires capital investment – but where it is realized that only a proportion of the population who could buy a product actually do buy it. Market segmentation is the technique of establishing which types of customer buy your product and service, and which do not. Mobile phones are these days promoted as being handy objects for more sorts of individual than business tycoons.

### (iii) Diversification strategies

To diversify is the only way to fill up the planning gap for a company which is efficient and profitable, and has a comprehensive range of products and services in the widest possible range of markets. This is because there is no limit to the amount of diversification that can be undertaken in the long term. The concept was developed by Igor Ansoff. The alternative product/market strategies are shown in Figure 3.4.

Put simply, diversification is doing something different – not in place of existing products or markets, but in addition. Figure 3.4

**Figure 3.4**

| Product/market strategies | | |
|---|---|---|
| **Market sectors** | | |
| | Present markets | New markets |
| Present products | PRODUCT RANGE | MARKET EXPANSION |
| New products | EXPAND PRODUCT RANGE | DIVERSIFY |

**Product range** (row label for the lower left)

suggests that the Diversification box is limited. In reality there is nothing that could not be done under this category of strategic move.

Firms choose to diversify for a variety of reasons:

- It may be the only way of filling the planning gap. If your market is already global, your product range is comprehensive, and the company is profitable, then diversification is the logical growth path. The major oil companies of the world fit this category – where is growth to come from in such companies as Shell and Exxon?

- It may be a better alternative than expansion in terms of the return on investment. There are situations when to expand a market or the product range is so expensive and the potential benefits so small that little gain would accrue from so doing. To achieve the required increase in performance needs diversification. For example, a firm selling its products throughout North America may look at Europe as a potential market. The cost of getting into that market would be very large (since it is not a single homogeneous market, but many) and the risks would also be very high.

- Some firms diversify as an insurance policy. If the environmental scanning process suggests that tough times lie ahead in your existing markets, or your products are mature and may even be on the point of decline, it may be better to get another "string to your bow."

- Diversification is used at times as a way of using spare cash – if the firm is well managed enough to have a cashflow surplus then rather than simply invest the money, buy or set up another business.

- Finally some firms diversify for reasons that do not make strict business logic. The opportunity comes up to buy a business – or start one up – which appeals to the senior management. Richard Branson's "Virgin Cola" does not appear (apart from the name) to have much to do with records or airlines.

## *Types of diversification*

Diversification is often a logical extension of a company's current operations, where there is some connection with existing skills and knowledge. This book is published under the imprint of Pitman, with the name *Financial Times* in association. Both companies are owned by the Pearson Group. The two businesses have different markets (in the narrow sense), and the products are very different. Yet both are printed media firms. The "technology" and the "market" are *related* to each other.

At the other extreme there is the sort of diversification where everything is different and there is neither market, nor product relatedness. This is conglomerate diversification and Hanson plc is an excellent example, owning a variety of companies including the American Kaiser Cement company, Renison Goldfields in Australia, Imperial Tobacco, a coalmining firm (Peabody) and brickmaking firms in the UK. The only point of similarity is that they are what the company describes as "basic industries."

This type of diversification is not often popular with investors, because in effect the company has become a kind of investment trust – and many investors would prefer to build their own portfolios, investing for preference in companies which clearly specialize in particular types of activity. The investment decision with conglomerate diversification is slightly different to other forms in that no account needs to be taken of commercial or industrial logic, the accounting criteria are the paramount consideration. There is an increased risk, however, because there is a lack of knowledge of the existing business – its markets and its products; its future is uncertain. How do we know it will be a success?

## 6 Which type of strategy is best?

The short answer is that it all depends on the situation in which the company finds itself. One strong argument is that the company should adopt a policy of what Tom Peters and Robert Waterman have described as "Sticking to the Knitting: staying with the business you know."

Another is policy based on the principle of "widening the search" – gradually expanding further and further away from home base and core products, looking for ways of filling up the gap. This argument is supported by the view that risk rises the further away from "home" you jump.

Michael Porter's work on competitive advantage stresses that there are only two fundamental successful strategies: "low cost" or "differentiation." To have the lowest costs in the business gives considerable competitive advantage. This supports the view described above that being efficient and profitable in one's existing operations is essential. Differentiation implies doing things in a sufficiently superior way to the competition that you can command a premium price. Every sector of business has its Rolls Royce or its Gucci, its number one which sets the standard for the rest to follow.

The assumption is, of course, that the markets in which you operate actually have a future. On the other hand, the opportunities may be much greater in green fields. Recently, Gary Hamel and C.K. Prahalad argued that the way forward is actually to set out to recreate the market by, for example, finding new ways of delivering the products or services to the customers, or being able to tailor your goods to their precise needs. Home banking and insurance are good examples, as is shopping by Internet using the home computer. This is "changing the rules of the game," and being so innovative that the competition is left behind. This is expansion of the product in dramatic and novel ways, but again requires considerable investment, energy, and faith, since the returns are by no means assured.

The choice of strategy depends, then, partly on the size of the planning gap and partly on the strengths and weaknesses of the company, and the threats and opportunities which may occur in the business environment. It also depends on the extent to which risk can be entertained and what funds are available for investment.

## 7 Make or buy your future?

Once the strategic route is chosen, the means of achieving it have to be decided.

There is a fundamental choice: develop the new activities

inhouse, buy an existing business which satisfies the criteria, or enter into a joint venture or a strategic alliance with another company. All three choices have merits and disadvantages.

Developing new activities inhouse is time consuming, can divert management focus from current activities, and there is no certainty of success. It is, however, easier to keep under control and often a cheaper solution.

Acquisition is quick, but more expensive, and care has to be taken over what is being bought. The "due diligence" stage of making sure there is nothing nasty in the woodshed is vitally important, even for minor acquisitions.

Joint ventures and strategic alliances have the advantage that the other partner can bring expertise or other attributes which you may not possess. Often the difficulty is finding the right partner. Once working successfully, such activities take on a life of their own and a problem which either "parent" may find is that the venture cannot be controlled in the same way as an ordinary operating subsidiary. However, the investment and the risks in both these activities are shared – but so are the rewards.

# 8 Counting synergy

Synergy has been described as the $2 + 2 = 5$ effect. In most strategies the idea is to add something to the existing business which boosts the overall results to a greater level than the individual units were achieving before. If Company A takes over Company B, selling a complementary range of products to the same market, synergy is achievable by rationalizing distribution, selling, and much administration. But there is a big danger. Often too much weight is given to the synergistic effects. Frequently it is difficult to know exactly what savings will be made and sometimes "negative synergy" occurs ($2 + 2 = 3$ or less). Great so-called mergers often come unstuck because there is no blending of strengths, just a collision of values, attitudes, systems, and culture.

# LAST WORD ON STRATEGY

The preliminary assessment of a variety of strategic options will give a view about how to fill the gap. The next part of the exercise is actually to carry out the calculations to judge which option will deliver the results everyone wants. *"Construct realistic strategies that don't require rocket science."* This is one of Jack Smith's "turnaround tips." (President and CEO, General Motors).

◆

If you could predict the future
there would be few problems in
managing a business.

◆

# Chapter 4

♦

# WHAT NEEDS TO BE FORECAST?

This chapter deals with the information you need to collect so that the process of formally evaluating whether or not it is worthwhile proceeding with the investment can begin. The information to look for will include:

- What kind of investment it is and comparison with the competition.
- Quantitative versus qualitative information.
- Market research.
- Estimating the level of sales, costs and capital expenditure.

# THE NATURE OF THE INVESTMENT

The process of strategy formulation opens up the discussion about the kinds of investment that need to be made in the business in the future. There are several different types of investment and these include:

- Investment in replacement assets needed to maintain a "best in class" position in the industry or to establish the lowest cost base.
- Defensive investment needed to sustain the present position in the market place, in particular, against competitors.
- Investment which leads to strategic flexibility – building capabilities for the future of the business – capabilities for future projects.
- Investment in leading edge technologies or products where no market currently exists in so-called disruptive technologies.
- Investment which is necessary because of legislative activity by governments – investment in health and safety, pollution controls and other environmental requirements.

Whatever the type of investment, we saw in Chapter 2 that there is a need for comparison with specific competitors within the industry, with what the best do or with the industry in general. In the process of the strategic audit, it was very useful to compare ourselves with the other businesses in our industry – preferably the "best in class." Comparisons can be made with levels of profitability, margins, growth rates and so on. From the point of view of this chapter, what is important about this benchmarking process is that it is clear that such comparisons, inevitably, lead us to think in quantitative terms.

# QUANTITATIVE AND QUALITATIVE INFORMATION

When it comes to the evaluation of strategies and comparison with other companies, "quantitative terms" specifically means "money terms." This is because it is easiest to compare companies using their accounting results which are, for the most part, expressed in money terms. For example:

Coca-Cola company makes more profit (or net income) than Pepsi-Cola.

Exxon makes a higher return on its capital than Mobil.

Tomkins plc has a higher growth in sales than Wassall plc (both firms are growing, UK-based, diversified industrial companies).

Each of the comparative figures in the examples above are able to be expressed in money terms. Profit or net income is calculated in financial accounts based on money values. Return is usually expressed as a percentage but of two monetary figures – profit divided by capital employed. Growth in sales also uses money values, although some industries refer to sales growth in terms of the growth in units sold – for example, the number of cars sold in the motor industry.

If the strategic analysis has thrown up the need for more investment, the required investment proposals are also evaluated – at least in the first instance – in quantitative, money terms. What this means is that investment proposals are initially evaluated by considering the parts of them which can be readily quantified. The problem is that it is very difficult to estimate the financial effect of the more qualitative aspects of an investment proposal. Consequently, only those items that are reasonably easy to forecast in money terms are included in the computations. For example:

- It is possible to estimate the demand for a new product through good market research and by statistical methods, but it may be very difficult to forecast the effect of the introduction of the new product on the demand for older products in the same product range. Consequently, the wider implications of the introduction of the new product are ignored in the initial financial appraisal.

- It may be relatively straightforward to estimate the unit costs of a new product, making assumptions about current productivity. In fact, because of the increased volume following the introduction of another product, overall productivity may improve or worsen. Productivity may increase because of greater efficiency – better use of overall resources – and worker morale may improve when they see the introduction of new products which might suggest to them continuity of employment. On the other hand, productivity may worsen if production lines become overloaded, too much overtime has to be worked, and so on.

The examples above show that it is difficult to measure the wider implications of a particular investment. Initial investment appraisal in quantitative terms tends, therefore, to take the project in isolation. The wider issues – how the project affects the remainder of the organization – are left to one side in the initial appraisal. The idea is that, given some figures, the proposal can be run through a financial screening process. If it looks like being worthwhile to proceed with the investment from this financial point of view, managers will take this fact on board and then consider the less quantifiable issues surrounding the investment proposal.

There may be many qualitative factors that need to be taken into account by the management team which is making a decision about an investment proposition We will discuss those issues in more detail later – specifically in Chapters 8, 9 and 10. Taking the wider issues into account but not attempting to quantify them is, after all, where the skill of management lies – taking decisions without concrete information and using managers' judgment.

Whichever figures are used as a basis for the investment appraisal, it must be remembered that the figures are *estimates* of what is expected to happen in the future. They have no certainty. Events will almost certainly shape the outcome of the investment so that it is quite different from the original expectations. This is a major difficulty in making investment decisions. We cannot be sure of the future and the risk of making the wrong assumptions originally may mean that we pursue strategies which are ultimately unsuccessful and reject strategies which would have been successful if only we had undertaken them.

Consequently, although the figures in the financial calculations may look accurate and fairly concrete, it must always be remembered that they are only based on management's assessment of what will happen in the future. A simple example based on the local branch of your bank may suffice to elaborate this point.

Many banks these days have a desk at which an investment adviser seeks to help customers with questions about their investments, savings plans, pensions and mortgage advice. A simple budget will help decide whether it is worthwile (that is, profitable) to have such a desk in a particular branch. All that you would have to do is work out the costs and compare that with the fee income the adviser might earn. The costs that would need to be estimated would be the adviser's salary, social security costs, pension, holiday pay, and attributable overheads, including stationery, telephone, and computer facilities.

But this is where the problem lies. Although we may be fairly certain about the costs involved here, the figures for fee income would very much be estimates (guestimates?). Only time will tell whether they are accurate. This means that there is some degree of uncertainty as to whether the branch of the bank should in fact employ a financial adviser. Although the figures may show a potential income of say £35,000 each year compared with costs of say £33,000 per year, the decision as to whether or not to create such a post at the bank has to be taken on the basis of an estimate of net income rather than certain knowledge of the future profitability of the post.

The point about the example of the bank's proposed strategy in providing more assistance (in a new area from the bank's point of view) is that the figures used in the analysis are based on the bank's best estimates of the outcome from their new strategy. They can be *fairly* certain about costs but they will be very uncertain about revenues. Will the investment be worthwhile?

So even the financial figures used in the appraisal of strategies are based on estimates. Thus they form only part of the decision-making process. The bank's managers will have to decide on the basis of the financial information together with any other pertinent information they have as to whether or not to employ the adviser. Two points should be clear in conclusion:

1 Costs and revenues, even if they can be identified, are essentially estimates of future outcomes

2 Other benefits or adverse features may be very difficult to quantify, so they are left out of the initial financial appraisal.

# MARKET RESEARCH

The aim of market research is to help a company find out more about its customers – what they want, what they like and dislike, and generally to try to identify what will lead them to buy from us rather than the competition. However, it has to deal with human nature, which adds a degree of uncertainty to the conclusions. It also has other limitations: it cannot always tell a company what new inventions should be introduced, or whether there is likely to be a continuing demand for some product or service currently on offer. For instance, if your company makes and sells bottled beer, market research can tell you:

- What your customers think of it.
- How it compares with other brands (in taste and cost and availability).
- What share of the market your products have.
- Whether the market appears to be growing.
- Whether new "tastes" are coming in.

On the other hand, market research cannot tell you:

- How much you will sell next year (or in ten years' time).
- What the competition will do to prices, advertising and new products in the future (they do not know themselves.)
- Whether some totally unknown company will come on the scene and capture your market with some innovative product.

The issue as far as the strategic decision is concerned is to try to assess what the likely demand will be for all of our products, both existing and planned, over the life of the project for at the end of the day, the most important element in the whole equation is: How many will be sold at a specific price and over what timescale?

---

**♦ POINT TO PONDER ♦**

**How did the Disney Corporation assess the likely demand at Euro Disney in France?**

---

# INFORMATION NEEDED FOR
# FINANCIAL ANALYSIS

The next few chapters describe the procedures used to evaluate strategies and the investment required for them from a financial point of view. Financial numbers are estimated for the outcome of future events. They are then put through a fairly formal numerical analysis. In this chapter we begin the overall evaluation process by outlining what has to be forecast in order to obtain the figures that are needed for the initial financial screening. We shall not only explain what information is required but also discuss how it may be obtained.

In very simple terms, "all" that has to be estimated when making a strategic investment decision are the following:

- the expected sales or revenues from the investment;
- the costs associated with such sales;
- the capital expenditure required in the making of the products or the provision of the service to achieve such sales.

It is important to realize that a considerable amount of work may be needed to obtain this information. Lines and lines of data will have to be forecast and estimated to the best of the ability of the market economists, engineers, cost estimators, management accountants, and so on.

Revenues and costs will have to be estimated *over the likely life* – or life cycle – of the product or investment concerned. Thus estimates of demand and of the consequential costs have to be made not only for one year but for many. Most people know how difficult it is to forecast what will happen in the year ahead, let alone further ahead than that. Get your friends to estimate today the price of a jar of instant coffee in one year's time. Some will be right, some will not! Yet it is this kind of estimate that we are making in a forecast of income and expenditure for a strategic investment – and for many years ahead.

Often the time taken to build budgets of this kind may amount to several man years. You may have been involved in collection or provision of data on sales revenues or on costs for a particularly large investment proposal. To find out about and provide the data that are required for a proper analysis of an investment decision is a heavily time-consuming process.

## Real examples of the effort required on pre-project work

- analysis of market needs for a new computer software
- costings for a large construction project
- estimates of the capital cost of an oil well or an oil pipeline
- estimates of the environmental costs (pollution controls, etc) and other running costs of a new chemical plant

An example of the time taken before a project actually reached its production stage is that of the development of the Troll gas field in the North Sea. The field was discovered in 1979. The construction of the production platform was begun in 1986 and was installed in 1995 with production commencing in 1996.

Remember the three categories of data that are needed are estimates of sales, costs and capital assets.

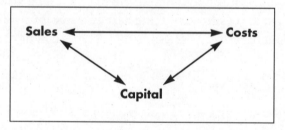

Which of these inputs to the decision is most important will almost certainly depend upon factors within the strategic decision that is being made. For example:

- If the project is demand led – that is where a product or service is developed to meet an observed customer demand – the critical success factor may well be whether the product can be produced at a cost from which a price can be derived with which customers will be happy. Product cost estimates will be most important in this case.

An example might be the expected cost of aluminium over the product life cycle of, say, a powerboat engine based on an aluminium engine block. Aluminium prices follow a cyclical pattern. The accuracy with which this cycle can be predicted will be of major importance to the success of the product.

- Where the ideas for the investment have developed from research and development but there is no clear demand for the product or service to be supplied, the critical factor will almost certainly be the forecast of the level of sales of the product. Market research and sales estimates will attempt to estimate the sales or revenue income from the investment.

  An example might be the development of a new rock band with some new music. The price at which the product is launched in the market will be critical to the success of the project, and can be estimated, but the volume of sales will be very uncertain.

- The sheer size of capital investment may be the overriding factor in the development of the product or service. Projects like North Sea oil wells and the Channel Tunnel are, or were, very dependent for their success upon the control of the initial capital investment costs involved. This is not to say that demand is unimportant – the price of oil is very important when one is considering an investment in an oil rig – but the vast initial costs of the investment are of primary importance in such investment decisions.

  An example of this type of investment is the development of a new (pharmaceutical) drug, which takes many, many years to develop and test. The main criteria in the analysis are the estimate of the development cost and the degree of certainty that eventually a safe product will be forthcoming.

# ESTIMATING REVENUES

The forecast of revenue to be earned from sales will be based upon estimates of demand for the product or service. Demand is expressed as the value of the new product that will be bought by users or consumers. That value of demand is affected by the quantity purchased and the price paid:

| Value of product sold | = | Total volume or quantity sold | × | price per unit of product |
|---|---|---|---|---|

So, in order to estimate demand, you need to consider two issues:

1 How much will be bought?
2 At which prices?

The quantity that will be purchased in a market will depend upon the total amount available to spend and relative prices. Consumers, whether they are individuals or business users, will have budgets to spend. The amount spent on any one product or service will depend upon their needs, the total amount they have to spend – their budgets – and the prices of other products and services they might consume. The equation is therefore very complex. In order to estimate how much of a particular product will be purchased, theoretically you have to know all about *all* the needs and preferences of potential customers, their income (how much they have to spend) and the prices of all other goods and services. Furthermore, businesses are working in a constantly changing environment because the number and types of firms in their industry grow or decline, technologies change, as do tastes, preferences and the levels of wealth of consumers. The term *effective demand* is often used in economics to explain the consumers' willingness as well as their ability to buy.

Understanding demand is essential for estimating revenues. You must know your customers and give them what they want – but

> **Understanding demand is essential for estimating revenues.**

also at prices that they are willing and able to pay. Furthermore, there has been a shift in business attitudes over the last five to ten years. Businesses no longer produce a product, albeit at a price, and then find out how many customers will buy it. Now the approach is to the customer, in the first instance, to find out what the customer wants – and then to supply a product to fulfill that requirement. If you think about it, this is actually far less risky, because a demand is established first and a product is made which then has a more certain market. However, this approach is not entirely satisfactory: where there are new technologies, for example, the demand may only be forthcoming when consumers realize, or are shown, what the new ideas can achieve. In this case, industry may have to take the lead.

# FORECASTING TECHNIQUES

There are various methods that can be used to forecast the level of demand for a new product. It may be possible to estimate the quantity of a product that might be sold into a market given a particular price. It is exceedingly difficult to establish much of an idea as to how much will be sold at *various* prices – that is, to estimate the whole demand curve for the product. Therefore, most forecasting techniques will provide estimates of likely volumes that will be sold, given a particular price:

1 **Market research surveys.** We expect you have at some time or another been approached either at home or at work or perhaps in the street with a request to answer a consumer survey questionnaire. The aim of such market research is to establish the level of demand for a particular product (or perhaps group of products) from the answers given by a random selection of the public. It is of course somewhat difficult to obtain a good random sample of people by street interviews because you are only likely to speak to people who happen to be walking along – what about all the motorists and cyclists? Consequently, telephoning questionnaires has become very popular, but even this method relies upon a suitable sample population being on the telephone and it depends upon the person answering the call.

   The problem with opinion research – as any review of the success of opinion polls to predict the results of a general election will support – is that it may not provide accurate, and therefore useful, information. Not only may you not be able to accept what people say when interviewed, but any time delay between the date of interview and the date of availability of, say, a new product may mean that there have been major changes in the marketplace. Furthermore, consumers and business clients may say they would like a product, but when it comes to buying it they may not be willing to do so.

2 **Estimating using expert opinion.** Managers of a supplying company may be asked their opinion about the likely volume of sales from their experience in and their knowledge of a particular market. The process may use the consensus of the personal insight of a number of managers – taking the average of their opinions or the overall opinion of a panel of them. If it is considered that particularly managers on a team are overwhelming, individual questionnaires can be completed and then analyzed by an independent party – the so-called *Delphi technique* (see Chapter 2).

3 **Trend analysis and projection into the future.** Formal forecasting techniques involve regression analysis and suchlike statistical measurements. The figures are based on past experience (actual data) from which a trend is identified. The assumption is that this observed trend will extend into the future.

This method may not be directly useful for a completely new product because there will not be any previous data. But consumer preferences and demand for similar products in the past may give some indication as to how the new product will do. Furthermore, very few products are entirely "new." There is usually some evidence which will be of use in forecasting what the future for a new product will hold.

4 **Market experimentation or "test marketing."** Many products, particularly consumer products, are initially tested in a small segment of the market in order to obtain some idea of what the overall demand for the new product would be in the economy as a whole. The virtue of such market testing is not only to establish the level of demand for the product, but also to obtain feedback on the product. Such feedback may well be used in the product development process to improve the final version and quality of the product eventually sold into the market at large.

One of the problems of forecasting in general and forecasting demand in particular is that we just do not know how good the forecasting technique is until some time after the event. Then of course it is too late; the investment has been undertaken and cannot easily be reversed. Even if an organization or a particular manager within it appears to be good at predictive consistency over a number of years there is absolutely no certainty that the forecasting models used by such an organization or an individual manager will be appro-

> **One of the problems of forecasting in general and forecasting demand in particular is that we just do not know how good the forecasting technique is until some time after the event.**

priate for future forecasting. It is all very difficult and we are sure that you are aware that if you could predict the future there would be few problems in managing a business.

## ESTIMATING COSTS

Hand in hand with estimating demand go the associated costs of meeting that demand. There is little point in establishing that there will be a demand for a product at a particular price, unless the product or service can be supplied at a cost that is commensurate with that price.

Although we have discussed estimating revenues first, it may be, of course, that cost drives our actions. We may discover, through good research and development, a cheaper or better way to make a product that is already available. In this case, we may be able to secure competitive advantage by undercutting competition and win market share through lower prices or improved quality or service or by having more product attributes for the same price.

Whether our sales are demand led or cost led, the detailed costs will have to be estimated. Just think what costs you would need to estimate if you were to introduce a new fruit juice onto the market. Excluding the cost of the processing plant, for the moment, consider the list of costs associated with the production of fruit juice.

### Costs associated with the production of fruit juice

- fruit from farmers, fruit growers
- sugar (if added)
- preservatives (if used)
- processing costs – power, labour, factory overheads
- packaging (including printing on packaging – which may need some design work – further cost)
- distribution costs
- marketing costs
- administrative costs – services, supplies, staff
- and so on

Even for such a simple product as a carton of fruit juice the degree of cost estimation is enormous. Just image what detail there would be for a more complex product – like a motor car, a computer system or a television set. And all the costs have to be estimated over the whole life of the investment strategy, that is, often for many years into the future.

# ESTIMATING REQUIREMENTS FOR CAPITAL ASSETS

Capital expenditure refers to the purchase of assets which will be needed for the production of the product or for the provision of the service decided upon by the strategy selected.

- Factory plant and machinery (e.g., car manufacturers' production lines).

- Equipment for the provision of a service (e.g., automatic teller machines in banks).

- Transport vehicles for distribution (e.g., lorries and trucks).

- Passenger transport vehicles (e.g., railway coaches for rail passengers).

The capital expenditure on such assets needs to be estimated so that their costs are brought into our calculations. All amounts should be included, in as great a level of detail as possible. For example, suppose you decide to build a house. The list of items to be included is surprisingly long – even down to such (expensive) things as garden landscaping. For each cost, you go and ask an expert or two for a quotation and make sure everything is accounted for, down to the last piece of turf in that landscaped garden.

# CAPITAL VERSUS REVENUE EXPENDITURE

In the case of a fruit juice producer, the plant and equipment required to pulp the fruit and extract the juice would be the main item. Factory premises could be leased, as could the trucks used to distribute the packaged product. Assets which are purchased are regarded as "capital" items and are treated differently from assets which are leased.

- Assets which are purchased are regarded as capital expenditure. The purchaser owns the asset.
- The lease charges for assets which are leased (from another owner) are regarded as revenue expenditure.

The importance of the difference between capital and revenue expenditure is in their accounting treatment. Capital assets are *depreciated* over their useful life and the depreciation is charged as a cost against income in order to calculate profit. Revenue expenditure in the form of lease payments is simply charged as a cost as and when it is incurred. The different treatments come to much the same thing:

---

**Depreciation charges (plus some allowance for the cost of interest on the capital required to purchase the asset)**

*will be much the same as*

**leasing costs from hiring the asset for use.**

---

As we shall see in Chapter 5, when a strategy requires a capital commitment, as it often does, the *cash flows* from the strategic investment are compared with this capital cost. This means that we do not have to concern ourselves with the depreciation charge. The cash flows from the investment amount to the revenues less cash costs before making any allocation for the depreciation cost of the asset. Cash flows from net income before charging depreciation over the life of the investment are compared with the capital cost of the investment.

# CONCLUSION

All this need for forecasting of revenues and of cost estimation connects very nicely, of course, with the need for a clear strategic plan in the first place. Strategic planning will identify the needs of the business and give some indication of the direction in which it can go. Forecasting demand for products and services which meet the strategic objectives and the associated costs will provide the first clues as to exactly how possible it is to achieve the strategic objectives set.

A final point should be made in this chapter. There may be a degree of self-fulfilling prophecy in an investment which pursues a particular strategy – if you are there, you may succeed, whereas, if you are not there, you cannot succeed. There is evidence that companies make sure they have a presence in a particular market just in case it takes off. Such investment may initially be expensive if the market is currently small or presently in recession, but the hope is that when things change, you will beat the competition by being ready to take advantage of the upturn in demand, before others can enter the market with their investment.

♦

Only when the investment has
been made and the actual
results begin coming in shall we
know how successful the
strategy has been. But the
decision has to be taken in
advance without the benefit of
such hindsight.

♦

# Chapter 5

♦

# CARRYING OUT THE FINANCIAL APPRAISAL

In Chapter 4 we showed that the forecast results of an investment strategy will be very much estimates of future demand and costs. Even the amount of the capital investment may be uncertain when the project is first being considered. Only when the investment has been made and the actual results begin coming in shall we know how successful the strategy has been. But the decision has to be taken in advance without the benefit of such hindsight.

In this chapter we shall be describing the computations that can be made based on the estimates of what will happen in the future. But calculations, because they are in a numerical form, always have the appearance of being accurate. Remember, however, that calculations in investment appraisal are based on forecasts. As we suggested in Chapter 4, and we shall again develop later, management judgment will also be very important.

There are nonetheless a number of techniques which form the basis of computations. The objective of these calculations is to see, at least from a quantitative point of view, whether the strategy that is being proposed appears to be worthwhile. In this chapter we:

- consider the concept of return on investment;
- describe and discuss payback;
- describe and discuss the two methods of discounted cash flow: net present value and internal rate of return.

# THE CONCEPT OF RETURN ON INVESTMENT

What exactly are these figures that will be the basis of the financial analysis? When it finally comes down to it all the work in estimating future sales revenue, related costs, overheads and the capital requirements will produce some sort of net income figure. This net income or net profit will be derived from the investment over a number of years and the objective of the analysis is to see whether the level of profit anticipated is sufficient bearing in mind the size of the investment.

For a company as a whole this concept of return on investment is often calculated as the return on capital employed. As we noted in Chapter 2, there are dozens of definitions of this term and therefore many ways of calculating it. A company has a level of profit which can be related with the capital employed in the business. The objective of calculating this ratio is to compare the company's return on capital with that of others. Table 5.1 sets out a summarized income account (profit and loss account) and balance sheet for a printing business – Best Printers Inc – based in the USA. The accounts are presented in the US format.

The big question is: is the net income of Best Printers sufficient, bearing in mind the amount of capital invested in the business? The operating profit is $2.4m for the year. The capital invested in the business equals the figure for total assets in the balance sheet: $17.0m. Thus, the *return* achieved by Best Printers for the year in question is 14.7 percent:

$$\text{Return on capital employed} = \frac{\$2.4m}{\$17.0m} = 14.7\%$$

This return on capital employed, from the point of view of Best Printers, is important for two reasons:

1 shareholders of the company are able to compare this return on capital employed with that of other companies. If Best Printers' return is not as high as other companies, shareholders may not be pleased and this will put pressure on the company's managers to improve profitability.

## Table 5.1

### The Financial Accounts of Best Printers Inc for the year to 31st December

| Income Statement | $000 |
|---|---|
| Net operating revenues | 25,000 |
| Cost of sales (labour, paper, inks, depreciation of equipment) | (15,000) |
| Gross profit | 10,000 |
| Expenses: Sales, marketing and distribution expenses | (3,100) |
| Administration expenses | (4,500) |
| Operating income | 2,400 |
| Interest expense | 200 |
| Income before income taxes | 2,200 |
| Income taxes | 650 |
| Net income | 1,550 |
| Dividends | 650 |
| Retained earnings | $900 |

| Balance Sheet | $000 | | $000 |
|---|---|---|---|
| **Assets** | | **Liabilities and Share-Owners' Equity** | |
| Current | | Current | |
| Cash | 650 | Accounts payable | 2,550 |
| Trade accounts receivable | 4,000 | | |
| Inventories | 2,100 | Long-term debt | 2,150 |
| | 6,750 | | |
| Plant and equipment | | Share-owners' equity | |
| Printing equipment, at cost | | Common stock, $.50 | |
| less depreciation | 10,250 | par value | 3,000 |
| | | Capital surplus | 4,050 |
| | | Reinvested earnings | 5,250 |
| | | | 12,300 |
| | $17,000 | | $17,000 |

2 the return on capital employed will set a target rate of return for new investment in Best Printers. Managers in the company will be wary of taking on projects with a forecast return that is lower than the company's current return on capital employed. This is because any lower returns from new investment will bring down the average for the whole company. In principle, Best Printers will not wish to undertake any major investment unless it can promise a return of 14.7 percent.

The concept of return is crucial to the investment decision. There is not really much point in saying that a company makes a particular level

**The concept of return is crucial to the investment decision.**

of net income from a project unless you say also how much is invested in the project. This is because the people who put up the finance for the project will expect a return on it.

The providers of finance might be:

- **the company itself** – investing cash reserves put aside for such investment
- **shareholders** – buying additional shares in the company to finance the investment
- **lenders** – such as banks or other lending institutions providing loans.

Each of these investors will require some form of return on the money invested in the new investment. If the company is investing its own cash a return on the investment will be required that is at least equal to the returns currently achieved by the company as a whole. If, for example, a company is making a 15 percent return, it will not wish to invest in a new project which only achieves a 12 percent return. If shareholders are buying additional shares in the company they will expect dividends and share growth on those new shares that are equally as good as they expect from the shares that they held in the company previously. Finally, if a company investing in projects borrows the money then the lenders to the company will expect a rate of interest to be paid.

Return needs to take into account the whole life of a strategic policy. The income "stream" over the whole life of an investment should be considered in calculating the rate of return. The net income for *a particular year* is not necessarily an indication of the success of

**Return needs to take into account the whole life of a strategic policy.**

the strategy. Net income may vary from year to year because of increasing or decreasing costs or sales demand or because of changes in prices. So the annual returns over the life of an investment may also vary. All the years of the investment should therefore be taken into account; it is the return achieved over the whole life of the investment that is important.

This need to assess the returns from a strategic investment over the whole life of the project poses some problems. The concept of return is an annual rate. If we are to consider the annual rate of return for each year of the investment, each individual year's rate of return may well vary quite considerably. What are we to do about this when we consider the rate of return for the whole investment? We could take an average of each year's individual rates of return, although this might not be too precise. There are, however, techniques which do take into account the variability of returns over the life of an investment very accurately. But, as we shall see these are not based upon income measures or upon average return on capital figures.

## INVESTMENT APPRAISAL TECHNIQUES

In order to develop the methods of financial appraisal techniques in some detail, let us take a very simple example of the investment of $50,000 in new print equipment by Best Printers Inc whose income statement and balance sheet was set out in Table 5.1. This amount of expenditure cannot be regarded as a "strategic" investment, as such, by Best Printers – although it may be part of the company's strategy to replace the equipment it has or to introduce new equipment over a number of years. The panel illustrates the decision that Best Printers face.

---

**♦ THE PRINTER'S DILEMMA ♦**

If you could set up as a printer with £50,000 worth of printing machinery, would you be interested in such a business if the income from that investment was expected to be £5,000 per year, but for just 5 years?

Assume that the amount of work that you would do with the printing equipment would mean that it would be completely worn out after five years and therefore valueless and would need to be replaced then. So the period over which our investment needs to be assessed is the full five years.

This is much the same question that the directors of Best Printers are facing as they decide upon the investment of $50,000 in new printing equipment.

---

There are several ways of looking at the proposed investment:

- return on capital;
- payback;
- discounted cash flow: net present value and internal rate of return.

# RETURN ON CAPITAL

The simplest way to look at the rate of return is to say that it amounts to 10 percent per year – the net income of £5,000 being expressed as a percentage of the capital investment of £50,000.

## Average return or gross return?

There is just one problem with this calculation. Here we have a depreciating asset – the printing equipment – which depreciates from an original cost of £50,000 to nothing at the end of five years. Consequently, we can argue that the average investment in the project is £25,000 – see Figure 5.1: The average return on investment. Assuming that the investment on average over its life is £25,000 comparing the £5,000 income per year we get an average rate of return on the project of 20 percent, rather than the 10 percent based on the gross value of the investment.

**Figure 5.1**

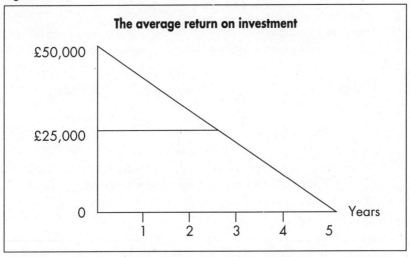

**The average return on investment**

£50,000

£25,000

0

Years

1    2    3    4    5

This puts our investment in a much better light. Although we have so far said nothing about the levels of return that are reasonably required on a capital investment you can see that a 20 percent return is very much better than a 10 percent return.

---

**♦ POINT TO PONDER ♦**

Consider, taking into account in the current economic climate in your country, what you would regard as being a reasonable return on the £50,000 or its equivalent?

---

We do know that the return on capital employed for the whole of Best Printers is 14.7 percent. This was based on the current year's profit divided by the total assets less current liabilities of the company. If the total assets include assets which are on average half way through their economic life and thus half depreciated, it is reasonable to compare the average return calculated for our project (20 percent) with the company's overall return (14.7 percent).

## Profit, depreciation and cash flow: the key difference

In accounting terms, the income of £5,000 per year for the five years of the project will take depreciation into account. (Depreciation is the accounting term which allocates the capital cost of an asset over its expected useful life.) If depreciation is assumed to be "straight line" (that is, the same amount each year), it will amount to £10,000 per year – £50,000 of capital investment depreciated equally over five years. If sales income from the project is expected to be £61,500 every year, the profit and loss account for the project might be as shown in Table 5.2.

**Table 5.2**

| Profit and loss account for the project, each year | |
| --- | --- |
| | £ |
| Sales revenue | 61,500 |
| Cost of sales (including depreciation of £10,000) | 42,400 |
| Gross margin | 19,100 |
| Directly attributable fixed costs | 14,100 |
| Annual income from project | £5,000 |

If we make a further assumption that all revenues and all costs, *excluding depreciation,* consist of cash receipts and payments in the year, the cash flow from operations can be shown to be £15,000 each year. See Table 5.3.

**Table 5.3**

| Cash flow from operations, each year | |
| --- | --- |
| | £ |
| Receipts from sales | 61,500 |
| Payments for cost sales, excluding depreciation* | (32,400) |
| Payments regarding directly attributable expenses | (14,100) |
| Cash flow from operations | £15,000 |

*Depreciation whilst being a charge in the calculation of profit is an allocation of cost, not a cash expense.

# PAYBACK

Imagine that you had borrowed the £50,000 from a bank over a three-year period. Ignoring for the time being any interest you would have to pay, would you be able to repay the bank in three years' time? Looking at Table 5.3 the answer is not quite, and the calculation works like this:

> The *cash flows* generated by the project amount to £15,000 per year and three years of cash flows equals £45,000, less than the £50,000 required by the bank. It would take 3⅓ years to pay back the loan, ignoring any interest earned on the cash set aside to repay the bank loan and ignoring any interest payable to the bank for providing the loan for the investment.

What we have done here is to calculate a simple *payback period*. Payback answers the question: How quickly does the project pay back the original capital invested in the project?

Payback is a very powerful tool in investment analysis. Most companies use it as a hurdle over which projects should be able to jump. The idea is that the quicker the firm gets its money back the better because the cash received can be reinvested in the business in further profitable investments.

**Payback is a very powerful tool in investment analysis. Most companies use it as a hurdle over which projects should be able to jump.**

However, great care should be taken in using payback because it has serious drawbacks:

- It completely ignores the cash flows and profits expected from the investment after the payback period. No one would have invested in the Channel Tunnel (the rail tunnel between England and France) because of the massive investment and the very long payback period of about 15 years unless some account was taken of the very high incomes expected after the payback period and of the very long period of the use of the tunnel after the payback period.

**Table 5.4**

### Payback comparing two projects

Cash flows estimated for two projects A & B (£m)

| Project | Capital cost | Year 1 | Year 2 | Year 3 | Year 4 onwards |
|---------|--------------|--------|--------|--------|----------------|
| A       | −10          | +6     | +2     | +2     | +2             |
| B       | −10          | +3     | +3     | +4     | +4             |

Each of these investments pays back £10m in three years

- Payback takes no account of the timing within the payback period. For example, in Table 5.4, the two investment proposals for the investment of £10m both have the same payback period.

  More of the cash flow is received in Project A in the early years as opposed to that received in Project B. It may be that Project A is preferred to Project B although it has to be said that the cash flows after the payback period are much higher in the case of Project B.

- The major problem with payback is not so much that it does not take into account the full length and timing of the income from the investment, but rather that there is no rationale for selecting a particular length of payback period. It might be useful where you want to know how soon you can repay a bank loan but simply to reject a sound investment proposal because it does not meet an arbitrary three-year payback can mean that you miss some very profitable opportunities in business.

We must emphasize that payback is used in practice by most companies particularly as an initial screening of the investment proposals made to the boards of companies. Different industry sectors will have different payback hurdles. Where the risks are the highest return will often be expected faster.

**Different industry sectors will have different payback hurdles. Where the risks are the highest return will often be expected faster.**

# DISCOUNTED CASH FLOW

Less obvious but the proper way to evaluate investments is undoubtedly to use discounted cash flow (DCF) techniques. This is because discounted cash flow is based on sound financial economic principles. DCF techniques take into account the full life of the investment and the timing of receipts and payments. The method compares cash flows received over the life of the project with the cash invested in it.

By way of example, we shall use DCF techniques on the proposed investment in printing equipment described above. It is most unlikely that DCF will be appropriate for such a short-lived invest-ment decision. This does not mean to say that DCF cannot be used in such a case, but rather that it is a bit too precise a method to use for such a small investment over such a short period. Discounted cash flow techniques are used more often in the following circumstances:

- An investment where activity will generate cash flows over more than five years.

- Investments of large amounts of capital expenditure, say over £1m. This does very much depend upon the particular rules per-taining to capital investment appraisal in a particular company. Most companies have or should have budgetary control limits on capital expenditure. Investments which need capital of more than a specific figure laid down by senior management will have to be passed through a formal process of evaluation.

- For projects where cash flows generated from a project are irregu-lar and therefore not of similar amounts from period to period. In such cases the averaging effect of return on capital employed is a very imprecise method of assessing the return on a project.

## Net present value

The fundamental basis of discounted cash flow techniques is founded on the principle of saying: Look, I am expecting a cash flow of £15,000 in a year's time. What is that equivalent to *now* if I take an interest rate into account?

Another way of saying this is: How much do I need to invest now at say 10 percent to become the expected amount of cash in a year's time? In the example of our printer's project, we are expecting £15,000 per year cash. Allowing for 10 percent interest the amount that we would have to invest now to be equivalent to £15,000 in a year's time is £13,636. This is because £13,636 plus 10 percent for one year equals £15,000. The calculation is set out in the panel.

---

**Net present value computations**

$$10\% \text{ of } £13,636 = \frac{\begin{array}{r} £13,636\ + \\ 1,364 \end{array}}{£15,000}$$

Another way of expressing this is:
$$£13,636 \times (1.10) = £15,000$$

*or*

$$£13,636 = \frac{£15,000}{1.10}$$

---

If we carry out this calculation for each of the £15,000 cash flows over the five years of the investment, what we will obtain is what is known as the *present value* of those future cash flows. The present value of £15,000 in one years' time (invested at 10 percent) is £13,636.

The present value of the £15,000 expected cash flow in *two* years' time is: £12,397. The mathematics for this is:

$$£12,397 = \frac{£15,000}{(1.10)^2}$$

That is, £12,397 invested now at a return of 10 percent will achieve a total value of £15,000 in two years' time. Putting this the other way round, £12,397 is said to be the present value of £15,000 to be received in two years' time – the interest in the first year is £1,240 and as this is reinvested, the interest in year 2 will be £1,364.

The process is known as *discounted* cash flow because the effect of finding a present value for a future cash flow is to reduce the expected future cash flow taking into account the interest rate. This reduction process is called discounting and thus discounted cash flows are those forecast cash flows which have been reduced to their present value.

The whole point about discounted cash flow is that these present values of future cash flows can be added up – they are each the equivalent present value of the cash flow expected in the future. The total of these present values can then be compared with the initial cost of the investment. Like is compared with like.

Basically what we are doing is calculating what is known as a *net* present value. We are netting off the initial investment against the sum of the present values of the future cash flows. If the net present value is positive then the project is acceptable at the rate of interest allowed for in calculating the present values. If the net present value is negative then the project has not achieved the rate of interest used in calculating the present values of the future cash flows. The net present value decision rule is:

---

### ◆ NET PRESENT VALUE DECISION RULE ◆

If the *total* of the present values of the future cash flows, allowing for the interest rate assumed in their calculation, is greater than the initial cost of the investment, then the overall return on the investment can be said to be greater than the rate of interest used in calculating the present values in the first place.

---

Table 5.5 shows that, using 10 percent as an interest rate, the net present value of the printing equipment project is positive.

If 20 percent is used as the interest rate, the net present value of the printing equipment project is negative. See Table 5.6.

In conclusion, if the printer is happy with a real rate of return of 10 percent then (other things being equal) the new equipment would be bought. If 20 percent is needed then the project gets the "thumbs down."

## Internal rate of return

It is much more usual to express the outcome of a project in terms of its *internal rate of return*.

**Table 5.5**

| | | |
|---|---|---|
| **Net present value at 10 percent** | | |
| | Cash flows | Present value using 10% |
| Year 0* | –50,000 | –50,000 |
| 1 | 15,000 | 13,636 |
| 2 | 15,000 | 12,397 |
| 3 | 15,000 | 11,270 |
| 4 | 15,000 | 10,245 |
| 5 | 15,000 | 9,314 |
| Net present value | | 6,862 |

*Conventionally, the investment which takes place at the beginning of year 1 is shown as taking place in "year 0"

**Table 5.6**

| | | |
|---|---|---|
| **Net present value at 20 percent** | | |
| | Cash flows | Present value using 20% |
| Year 0 | –50,000 | –50,000 |
| 1 | 15,000 | 12,500 |
| 2 | 15,000 | 10,417 |
| 3 | 15,000 | 8,681 |
| 4 | 15,000 | 7,234 |
| 5 | 15,000 | 6,028 |
| Net present value | | –5,140 |

There is a particular rate of interest which will make the total of the present values of future cash flows just equal to the capital investment. This is known as the internal rate of return. It is a sort of break-even rate of interest. In Tables 5.5 and 5.6 the 10 percent net present value is positive but using 20 percent the net present value is negative. Therefore the real internal rate of return is greater than 10 percent but less than 20 percent. But what is the actual internal rate of return? What rate of return will cause the present value of the future cash flows to equal the initial capital cost of the investment?

It has to be found by trial and error – by discounting the future cash flows at various rates of interest until the sum of the present values obtained thereby just equals the capital cost of the investment. Computer spreadsheets these days make the task much easier because the internal rate of return can be obtained there by using a formula.

In the example of our proposition to go into a printing business, the internal rate of return on the investment is 15.24 percent. If this rate of interest is used to calculate the present values of the future cash flows the net present value of the project is 0, as shown in Table 5.7.

**Table 5.7**

| The internal rate of return | | |
|---|---|---|
| | Cash flows | Present value using 15.24% |
| Year 0 | –50,000 | –50,000 |
| 1 | 15,000 | 13,017 |
| 2 | 15,000 | 11,295 |
| 3 | 15,000 | 9,802 |
| 4 | 15,000 | 8,505 |
| 5 | 15,000 | 7,381 |
| Net present value | | 0 |

So we can now simply say that the return on the project is 15.24 percent. Most managements use the internal rate of return. It is much easier to say that the return on an investment is such and such a percentage. If net present value approach is used you have to say something along the following lines: Allowing for an interest rate of 10 percent, the net present value of the project is positive.

## Net present value and internal rate of return compared

If the net present value approach is used, managers are establishing whether or not the cash flows expected from a strategic proposal achieve the return they require from an investment. The present value of each year's cash flow is calculated using this required rate of return and then the total of the present values of the cash flows is compared with the initial cost of the investment.

If the internal rate of return is calculated, that rate is compared with the return required by managers. If the internal rate of return is higher than the required rate of return, the argument is that the project should proceed. If it is lower then the project should be abandoned.

In either case – the use of net present value or internal rate of return – it is clear that the required rate of return is central to the investment decision. Putting a figure upon that rate is very complex and is something that we discuss at length in Chapters 6 and 7. The rate of return required by managers of an enterprise depends upon:

- the company's present rate of return;
- the risk of the investment;
- the cost of capital to the investor;
- the levels of capital to the investor;
- the levels and incidence of taxation;
- the extent to which the proposal is a strategic fit.

# CONCLUSION

This chapter has outlined the techniques that accountants and other managers use to evaluate the strategic investments that are proposed. The trouble with these methods of appraisal is that they look very precise – and do indeed give very "accurate" answers in a numerical sense. But these very precise figures are based – as we indicated in Chapter 4 – on many, many assumptions. Those assumptions are estimates and forecasts about future activity, which is far from certain, so the likely outcome from strategic investment will probably be quite different from the computed values that we have shown in this chapter. Exactly how this problem of uncertainty about the actual results is dealt with in the strategic investment decision is dealt with in the next chapter.

♦

Risk or uncertainty is the
expression we use to describe
that concern we have when
setting budgets that the
expectations – and hopes –
about the future of the business
may not be achieved.

♦

# Chapter 6

◆

# HOW DO WE COPE WITH UNCERTAINTY?

The term "uncertainty" or "risk" in budgeting expresses what we all know in business – that things often do not turn out quite how we originally thought they would. In fact, it could be said that there would be no "fun" in managing an enterprise if all we had to do was to budget and that was that. As we saw in Chapter 2, the business environment is likely to upset the "best laid plans." Reacting ad hoc to those actual events which take us away from the planned path is what makes management interesting and absorbing. In this chapter we discuss how risk can be measured and whether or not the extra return for taking risk is enough.

> **Reacting ad hoc to those actual events which take us away from the planned path is what makes management interesting and absorbing.**

## CAPITAL BUDGETING AND RISK

Risk or uncertainty is the expression we use to describe that concern we have when setting budgets that the expectations – and hopes – about the future of the business may not be achieved. When even budgetary targets are set many assumptions have to be made. We all know that for many reasons the revenues and costs that have been budgeted will be different when the actual results are known. This may be because the assumptions we made about future levels of activity and costs were wrong or that some events occurred which were unforeseen:

- Sales of goods and services could be more or less than expected.
- Costs could be higher or lower than budgeted.
- Productivity levels could be better or worse than forecast.
- The general economic and business climate might be better or worse than expected.
- Technologies might change to alter the revenues or costs from those anticipated in the original budget.
- Prices of specific goods and services may be different than expected – or general inflation may be different than forecast, so that prices in general are different than were expected.

Conventional budgeting in most companies seeks to estimate the profitability of the business over a number of years ahead. This process is carried out in detail for no more than one or two years ahead. But still the actual events during that period will be such that the business is blown off course. Managers may well attempt to keep to budgetary targets by taking corrective action to get the business back on track – or they may decide to ignore the original plans and reforecast future profitability by resolving to follow a revised plan for the remainder of the next year or two.

When it comes to the evaluation of capital investment required in strategic planning, the period over which we are budgeting for is anything between five to fifteen years or more. In this case, over such a long period, there is plenty of time for events to change so that the results from the investment are very different from those which were originally expected. Furthermore, having undertaken the route of a strategic plan, it may not be too easy to change direction. Capital investment, once decided upon and undertaken, cannot be reversed. The most we can do is make the best of a difficult situation if actual events do not measure up to original expectations.

**Capital investment, once decided upon and undertaken, cannot be reversed.**

The term risk in the appraisal of capital budgets – and in the assessment of strategic plans is used to express the uncertainty about the future – the fact that things may not turn out as originally expected. What is required ideally is some *measure* of the degree of uncertainty about future results from a capital investment. At least then managers can see whether or not the returns for taking extra risk are sufficient. This is the assumption that is made: Investors may be interested in accepting risk in their investment, provided they can expect a higher return thereby.

# MEASUREMENT OF RISK

As we saw in Chapter 5, the *cash flows* expected from an investment are pre-eminent in assessing whether or not a particular project should be pursued – at least from the financial point of view. But what if those cash flows are uncertain? What happens if the cash flows anticipated are not forthcoming? It may well be that the cash flows are somewhat different than originally expected. How do we handle this in the process of investment appraisal? How did Shell work out that the cash flows from the Troll field will be high enough to justify the huge capital cost?

Risk itself is in fact defined in a *financial* context in a very precise way. Financial economics defines risk as:

> **the expected or forecast variability of outcome.**

When we undertake an investment we expect that there will be differences between the actual results and those originally envisaged – as will almost certainly be the case. We are effectively anticipating that future outcomes will *vary* from plan. So what is often included in the proposal for a large capital investment is an indication of the range of likely returns. The proposal might say that the return expected from an investment will be between 10 percent and 20 percent although the most likely return will be 15 percent. To say this may not appear to be very helpful, because the information implies that any particular return is not certain. It does give some idea of the *amount* of variability of return that is potentially possible in the return on the investment.

The point has already been made that the internal rate of return expected from an investment is based on forecasts of future cash flows over the whole life of the investment. If changes are made to those forecasts, the internal rate of return will change accordingly. Take the example of an investment which has an expected internal rate of return of 10 percent. All sorts of changes to the assumptions used in calculating that rate of return could be made.

- Sales levels could be increased or decreased by, say 5 percent or 10 percent.
- Running costs could be included at 5 percent or 10 percent more or less.
- Capital costs could be 5 percent or 10 percent more or less.

**Table 6.1**

| £000s | Best Guess | Costs + 10% | Sales + 10% | Capital + 10% |
|---|---|---|---|---|
| Sales | 500 | 500 | 550 | 500 |
| Costs | 400 | 440 | 400 | 400 |
| Profit | 100 | 60 | 150 | 100 |
| Capital cost | 1,000 | 1,000 | 1,100 | 1,000 |

**The effect of variations in expectations**

A glance at the profit line in Table 6.1 shows that the "worst" picture has a profit of only £60k on what could be an £1,100k investment. On the other hand profit could be £150k on the £1,000k investment.

By way of a more detailed example of how the degree of variation might be expressed, consider a project relating to the investment in production equipment which will manufacture plastic security cards (rather like the shape and size of a credit card). The equipment will produce cards to the specification of customers and the investment has the characteristics shown overleaf.

The internal rate of return of this project is 10 percent. Table 6.2 shows what the effect might be of making changes of ±5 percent and 10 percent to revenues, costs, and capital cost on the internal rate of return (IRR). As indicated in Table 6.2, if revenue is in fact 10 percent more, the IRR increases to 30 percent. If the costs paid out *decrease* by 10 percent the IRR increases to 27 percent and so on.

---

**Security card production equipment**

- Its life is 5 years.
- Capital cost is £200,000.
- Revenue cash receipts are expected to be £300,000 each year.
- Manufacturing costs – paid in cash – are expected to be £247,240 each year.

---

**Table 6.2**

| | | | | |
|---|---|---|---|---|
| **Making changes to original estimates** | | | | |
| *Revised returns based on following changes** | | | | |
| | +10%<br>change | +5%<br>change | –5%<br>change | –10%<br>change |
| Original estimates<br>changed | | | | |
| Revenue | 30 | 21 | –2 | –16 |
| Costs | 27 | 19 | 0 | –11 |
| Capital costs | 14 | 12 | 8 | 6 |

Note: Return based on the original estimates is 10 percent

*A positive change for revenue means more sales. A positive change for costs means lower costs. Vice versa for the negative changes.

## Risk measurement computations

Table 6.2 shows in a systematic way the changes that might occur in the original estimates of revenue, costs and capital expenditure in order to see what effect these might have on the expected project returns. It gives, in numerical form, a very good idea of the degree of variation in returns brought about by change in the original project estimates. The importance of defining risk in this way becomes apparent when it is shown that such variability can be *measured*.

Measurement of risk can take the form of looking at the effect of various changes in assumptions, as shown in the example of Table

105

6.2, or it may take the more formal (mathematically speaking) form of calculating a statistical measure of risk. There is a method – known as the *standard deviation* – which measures the expected amount of variation either side of the average return. The Appendix to this chapter shows how a standard deviation of returns may be calculated, based on the figures shown in Table 6.2 – and states what assumptions need to be made in order to calculate it.

The key benefit of the standard deviation is that it can be calculated and that it may then be used as a measure of variability. Its special characteristic is that it can be said that there is a 95 percent chance that the actual return achieved from the project will be within two standard deviations of the expected result. (This does make the assumption that the range of possible expected returns are "normally distributed.") Thus, as the standard deviation of expected returns calculated in the Appendix is 5.48 percent, we can say that there is a 95 percent chance that, whatever the actual return achieved is, it will be within ±10.96 percent (2 × 5.48 percent) of the expected return of 10 percent, which is the expected return in this case.

## An example of risk evaluation

Why is all this so important? Assume that part of the expansion strategy of a health club is to add a swimming pool to its facilities – something which it does not have at present. The club has to choose between building an outside, open air pool and an indoor pool. The return expected from the outside pool will be more certain and is expect to be 10 percent. The return on the indoor pool will be more risky, but the return is expected to be 15 percent. All other things being equal and ignoring risk, it seems that the health club should build the indoor pool because it has the higher return. However, adding knowledge about the risk of each investment could cause us to reconsider such a decision.

Let us say that the outdoor pool could do very well, but, because its season is limited, the very best return it could achieve is 20 percent. On the other hand, the worst return it could be expected to make is to achieve no return at all: 0 percent. If the indoor pool were to be used by club members much more than expected, it may be assumed that the project could make a 45 percent return – a very big return indeed. If the indoor pool was a failure and not liked by members for some reason, that investment might perform very badly and the investment could lose 15 percent. This situation is illustrated diagramatically in Figure 6.1.

The decision as to which pool to construct is now much more complex. While the expected return on the indoor pool project is 15 percent, it is possible that we could lose quite a bit of money from undertaking this investment. Therefore, we may be happier undertaking the openair pool where the expectation is that even in the worst circumstances, we will lose no money.

**Figure 6.1**

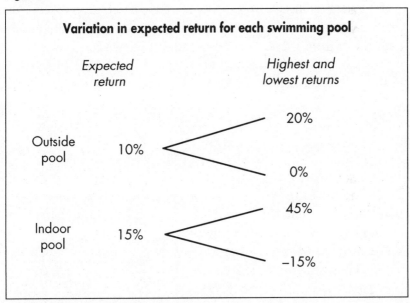

*If your money was at stake – which would you go for?*

The difference between the *expected* returns of the two investments is, of course, 5 percent. The question is: Is the extra 5 percent return that we are likely to get from the indoor pool project sufficient to compensate for the risk of possibly achieving something quite different than the 15 percent that is the most likely result? In this case, we may even lose 15 percent each year. Nonetheless, the most likely return from the indoor pool project is 5 percent more than from the outside pool. What we have here is a *premium* for taking additional risk. The risk premium in this case amounts to 5 percent – the extra return we hope to get investing in the indoor pool rather than the outdoor pool.

Whether or not the risk premium is adequate is yet another subjective decision that one has to make about investment decisions. There is no magic formula which tells us whether the extra return for accepting a wider range of possible returns is, in fact, worth the risk. All that can be done is to offer the information to the decision-takers when the proposed investment is being considered. The information about risk – the possible degree of variability in the expected returns – will be weighed with all the other information, financial and otherwise, before a decision is made.

But first, how do we estimate the degree of variation in expected returns from an investment? It is difficult enough to estimate the cash flows from the most likely scenario! How such variations in return are measured and included in the investment proposal is dealt with in the remainder of this chapter, after a note about the use of payback in the context of risk.

# PAYBACK

When we are aware that we have a fairly risky investment it may be comforting to know just how quickly the capital cost of the original investment is recovered. This is indicated by the payback period. Remember that payback simply measures the length of time it takes for incoming net cash flows to equal the capital cost of the investment. If an investment appears to be particularly risky it will be encouraging to know that the investment is at least expected to recover the capital cost in, say, three or four years. In the case of the two investments in swimming pools that were illustrated in Figure 6.1, the risk of the indoor pool project may have been too high for managers to accept – even though it had a higher return. But if those managers knew that the project's payback was only two or three years based on the most likely cash flows, this might have weighed the decision in favor of accepting the indoor pool project.

A little care has to be taken here however because the reverse is not necessarily true. A project with a very long payback period is not necessarily a risky investment. Large building or construction projects often have a very long payback period but are no more risky than the investment in a new consumer product which is expected to pay back quickly but may or may not be successful.

# ESTIMATING VARIATION IN EXPECTED CASH FLOWS

There are a number of ways which have been used over the years to provide some idea of the expected variation from the most likely cash flows from an investment. These are:

- the scenario approach;
- sensitivity analysis;
- simulation.

Let us look at each of these in turn.

# SCENARIO APPROACH

Scenarios are used at two levels in strategic investment evaluation. As we saw in Chapter 2 (p 41), scenarios are used to help choose the strategic direction of the company.

The futurology approach is mathematically based and attempts, using some complex modeling techniques, to assess what the world will look like many years ahead. The use in strategy is that it makes predictions of the big picture. For example, it may predict that the population of Italy is likely to fall significantly over the next fifty years. If you manufacture babyclothes, Italy may not be your favored market.

Scenario planning other than using futurology, as we saw in the case of the commodity buyer (p 41), tries to visualize what might happen in the company's world which will affect sales or the cost base in some significant way. A scenario approach may incorporate a modeled view, but often it is used to answer the question: What might happen? The strategic direction of the firm can be set bearing in mind that diametrically opposed futures may emerge – contingency plans have to be established to cover these eventualities.

Once a decision has been taken to invest in a particular strategic activity, then the second use of scenarios emerges – it can be used to link into specific aspects of the investment. Often the method is to identify the major variables in an attempt to assess what might affect the costings and forecasts which have been built into the original estimate. For example, it might be said:

- Volume sold could differ significantly from the estimates because there is a chance that such-and-such may happen – for example, competition may increase or collapse.

- Key costs (wages or materials or key components) could rise or fall because certain events might happen radically to change our best estimates.

The value of spending time imagining what might happen is that the visions that are created about the future provide a basis for the more precise form of calculation of alternative returns – sensitivity tests.

**The value of spending time imagining what might happen is that the visions that are created about the future provide a basis for the more precise form of calculation of alternative returns – sensitivity tests.**

# SENSITIVITY ANALYSIS

The aim of sensitivity analysis is to show the effect of differing assumptions about the various factors which create the cash flows of the project. Whereas the scenario asks "what might change" sensitivity asks: "by how much?" In its simplest form, a capital investment project can be reduced to:

- a capital sum invested initially;
- a stream of revenue receipts over the life of the investment;
- a stream of cash costs over the life of the project.

Sensitivity analysis aims to show the impact of variations in any of these elements of the capital investment appraisal upon the return expected to be achieved.

For example, changes could be placed on the assumptions that were made when estimating sales receipts. You could look at what would be the effect of, say, a 10 percent higher or lower price for the product or service supplied. Or you could consider what would be the effect of, say, 10 percent more or less in the volume of sales achieved; or the impact of a shorter or longer life on the return on the investment will be calculated.

One line of approach shows the effect of a percentage change in the assumptions used to make the original cash flow estimates; changes can be made to each element of the overall cash flow computations. An alternative approach would be to see by what percentage an element of the cash flow computation – capital, revenue or costs – could change before the return on the project was, say, 10 percent. Thus, if the internal rate of return of a project was 15 percent, you could show by what percentage sales prices or volumes could change before a minimum IRR of, say, 10 percent was achieved. There are two main methods of carrying out sensitivity analysis:

1 Showing what the effect of a certain percentage more or less would be on the overall return expected from the project.

2 Indicating by how much a particular figure in the calculation can alter before the return on the investment becomes 0 percent (or a preselected percentage return).

Table 6.3 shows an example illustrating the difference between the two approaches. The table uses the information about the security card manufacturing equipment used as an earlier illustration in Table 6.2. Further information about that product is as follows:

---

### Security card production equipment

- The annual revenue from the equipment is expected to be £300,000 representing 200,000 cards priced at £1 each.

- The manufacturing cost of £247,240 per year for those 300,000 cards are expected to be made up as follows:

  | | |
  |---|---|
  | Materials | £166,910 |
  | Labor | £51,620 |
  | Overheads | £28,710 |

- The capital cost of the equipment needed for the project is £200,000 as before and it is expected to last for 5 years.

---

Table 6.3 shows that if either product prices or volumes are 10 percent higher than forecast, the IRR of the project will be 30.4 percent rather than the expected 10 percent. If prices or volumes are 10 percent lower, the project will make an annual loss of 16.3 percent per year. A 10 percent reduction in material costs will mean that the return on the project is 21.7 percent. A material cost increase of 10 percent will mean the project will lose 3.3 percent per year. And so on.

**Table 6.3**

| Sensitivity analysis | | | |
|---|---|---|---|
| | IRR after 10% change | | IRR becomes 5% after |
| Original estimates changed | Positive effect | Negative effect | % change in estimate |
| Revenue | | | |
| Price* | 30.4 | −16.3 | 2.2 |
| Volume* | 30.4 | −16.3 | 2.2 |
| Cost | | | |
| Materials | 21.7 | −3.3 | 3.9 |
| Labor | 13.8 | 6.1 | 12.7 |
| Overheads | 12.1 | 7.8 | 22.9 |
| Capital costs | 14.3 | 6.4 | 14.2 |
| Notes: Return based on original estimates is 10 percent | | | |

*Both price and volume changes affect IRR in exactly the same way if inter-relationships between price and volume are ignored.

The alternative approach to sensitivity analysis is to see by how much variables in the decision can change before a particular level of return is achieved. This return is usually the minimum acceptable return on the project and in Table 6.3 that rate of return has been selected as 5 percent. The table shows by what percentage each factor of the investment decision can change before the project's return is as low as 5 percent. Product prices or volumes can fall by only 2.2 percent. Materials cost can increase by no more than 3.3 percent. But labor costs can increase by as much as 12.7 percent; and so on.

A graph may be derived showing the effect of a whole range of differing percentages of change in particular variables in the decision-making process. Figure 6.2 shows graphically how information about the effect of changing assumptions about the values of variables may be presented in this way. Figure 6.2 shows that the most sensitive variables in the calculations of this example are sales price and volume followed by material costs. Changes in the labor costs, overhead costs and in the capital cost of the project in this case have

**Figure 6.2**

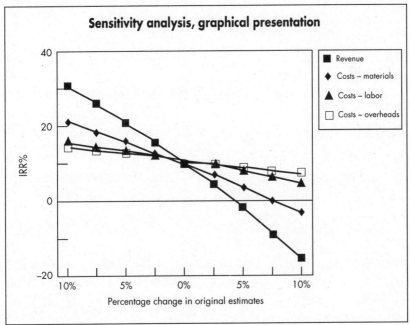

much the same effect on the outcome of the project – that is, not much effect on the return on the project. The labor and overheads cost lines and the capital cost line are much flatter than the others – indicating that there is relatively little change in the expected return if these costs are more or less than was originally planned.

This is all very well and may look very appropriate, but we have to make the point again that we are looking at the future and that all such estimates are just that – estimates. The process described in Chapter 5 to obtain just the most likely results involved much analysis and hours (months?) of work. The rather mechanistic approach used above to establish the sensitivities of the project to changing assumptions might appear scientific – and gives spuriously accurate figures – but a great deal more work would need to be carried out in practice to obtain realistic figures for the expected effect of increasing prices or increasing costs of raw materials and so on. Although the figures – and charts – so obtained may appear useful to the decision-making process, we may just be adding a degree of sophistication which is difficult to justify. It may be very difficult to quantify the effects of changes in the variables with any degree of accuracy. Therefore any further guesswork in the process of the evaluation of strategies may further undermine management's belief in the process of trying to assess strategies quantitatively at all.

## An example of a sensitivity analysis

Euro Disney used sensitivity analysis in their prospectus for the issue of share capital in 1989. They set out the effect of changes in:
- attendances*
- spending per capita
- delay in the opening
- construction cost
- resort and property development income
- inflation
- interest rates
- valuation of the Company in 2017

*an "attendance" represents one visitor visiting for one day. Thus a person visiting the park for three days would equal 3 attendances.

A copy of *part of* the sensitivity analysis undertaken by Euro Disney published in their 1989 prospectus is shown in Table 6.4. The Euro Disney prospectus included forecast results for almost 25 years ahead – from the anticipated opening in April 1992 to March 31 2017. The effect of sensitivity analysis on the return on capital (IRR) is shown, together with two alternatives: the effect of the forecasts on shareholders' dividends at various dates into the future and the effect on the anticipated value of each share in 1993.

The company's original projections were based on a financial model outlined in the prospectus, which included estimates of the number of people that would visit the park, their spending per head, operating expenses, and the capital costs of constructing the park. The prospectus also included estimates of revenues and costs related to the hotels and other commercial property on the site.

## Euro Disney

We now know, of course, what the actual attendances at the Park have been. In the first three years attendances were much less than the figures for reduced attendances assumed in the sensitivity figures. The sensitivity analysis indicated the effect of lower attendances of approximately 9 percent less – 10 million rather than 11 million in the first year. Furthermore, in the original forecast these attendances were expected to grow by 4.9 percent for the years 1993–6, but actual attendances grew much less than this. The actual attendances for 1994 showed no growth but rather a decline over 1993's figures:

Comparative attendances (millions days)

|  | 1992 | 1993 | 1994 |
|---|---|---|---|
| Original forecast | 11.0 | 11.5 | 12.1 |
| Forecast effect of reduced attendance | 10.0 | 10.5 | 11.0 |
| Actual attendance | 8.2 | 9.8 | 8.8 |

## Table 6.4

### Euro Disney sensitivity analysis

This table illustrates the projected returns to the investor based on the assumptions described in the prospectus and demonstrates the effect on these returns of variations in certain of the key assumptions. At the end of the period the company is assumed to be capitalized at 12.5 times net profit available for distribution in the year ending March 31 2017.

| | Net dividend per Share Years beginning April 1 | | | | | | Net value in April 1993* | Internal rate of return |
|---|---|---|---|---|---|---|---|---|
| | 1992 | 1995 | 2001 | 2001 | 2011 | 2016 | 1993* | |
| | | | | (FF) | | | (FF) | % |
| Company's original projections | 1.6 | 5.3 | 10.3 | 14.8 | 19.9 | 33.6 | 131 | 13.3 |
| (i) Reduced attendance | 1.6 | 5.3 | 9.4 | 13.8 | 18.4 | 31.7 | 119 | 12.7 |
| – assuming 10 m visits in the first year of operations of the MAGIC KINGDOM | | | | | | | | |
| (ii) Increased attendance | 1.6 | 5.3 | 11.1 | 15.9 | 21.3 | 35.6 | 141 | 13.8 |
| – assuming 12 m visits in the first year of operations of the MAGIC KINGDOM | | | | | | | | |
| (iii) Reduced per capita spending | 1.6 | 4.8 | 8.9 | 12.9 | 17.4 | 30.3 | 112 | 12.3 |
| – assuming per capita spending at both theme parks is lower by 10% | | | | | | | | |
| (iv) Increased per capita spend | 1.6 | 5.3 | 11.6 | 16.6 | 22.3 | 37 | 147 | 14.1 |
| – assuming per capita spending at both theme parks is higher by 10% | | | | | | | | |
| (v) Delay | 1.6 | 4.5 | 9.7 | 12.6 | 21.8 | 33.6 | 122 | 12.8 |
| – assuming a six-month delay in the opening of the MAGIC KINGDOM | | | | | | | | |
| (vi) Increased construction costs | 1.6 | 5.3 | 10.2 | 15.1 | 20.4 | 34 | 129 | 13.2 |
| – assuming costs of construction of Phase 1A are higher by 10% | | | | | | | | |
| (vii) Reduced resort and property development income | 1.6 | 5.3 | 9.8 | 14.3 | 19.3 | 33 | 126 | 13.0 |
| – assuming that income from all resort and property development is lower by 10% | | | | | | | | |

Source: Euro Disney prospectus 1989

*Net value in April 1993 reflects gross dividends per share and assumed residual value in 2017 discounted at an illustrative rate of 12%

With hindsight, we can see that the lower estimates of attendances were not low enough. It would have been interesting to see the results produced by Disney's financial model of attendances being around 30 percent less than expected! Euro Disney's charts are an excellent example of how the results from a sensitivity analysis may be presented. But the degree of sensitivity envisaged in the analysis did not, in the event, encompass actual results. Carrying out sensitivity analysis does not mean that actual results will be within the parameters envisaged in the best and worst cases!

## Inter-relationships

Sensitivity analysis looks at one change in the input information at a time, but the full ramifications of a particular change cannot readily be foreseen. There are inter-relationships involved. For example, if sales prices are increased by 10 percent, we cannot be sure that this will not have an opposite, adverse effect on sales volume. The overall effect may not be that an additional 10 percent will be earned in revenue. Similarly, when it comes to costs, if cost cutting is undertaken and, for example, wages are expected to be 5 percent less, we cannot be sure that quality is maintained and that there will be no adverse effect on sales thereby. So sensitivity analysis looks spuriously accurate but may very well not be as computationally sound as it appears at first sight.

**Sensitivity analysis looks at one change in the input information at a time, but the full ramifications of a particular change cannot readily be foreseen. There are inter-relationships involved.**

# SIMULATION

Simulation is a computer-based technique which *combines* the effect of variations that are possible in the factors which go into the calculation of cash flows. What is actually done in its simplest form is that a distribution of expected values is estimated for each input variable. For example, the price of the product or service may be expected to be £100 but it may be estimated that the price could be as much as, say, £120 or as little as £80. A distribution of expected values may be built up between these extremes using management's estimates of the likelihood of the various values between £120 and £80. Once a normal distribution is built up for each of the factors in the cash flow calculation, the computer program will work out a simulation of the expected overall return and the variations either side of it.

What is obtained is a normal distribution of the expected returns. If the standard deviation is 6 percent, one could say that while the most likely expected return is, say, 12 percent there is a 95 percent chance that any actual result will be between 24 percent and 0 percent (12 percent ±6 percent × 2).

Once again, it must be emphasized that the figures so obtained look as if they are accurate. They are, however, based on estimations of expected results and the anticipated possible variation either side of such results.

# ADDING PROBABILITIES TO SCENARIOS

A further level of the sophistication which may help in evaluating the degree of risk is to attach probabilities to various scenarios. It is to that aspect of the evaluation of projects that we now turn.

Managers assessing a project can be asked to attach various probabilities to the particular scenarios. For example, the most likely scenario could be given a weighting of 60 percent – that is, it is 60 percent certain that it will happen. Alternatively it may be that there is only a 10 percent chance of achieving an optimistic scenario but a 30 percent chance of achieving a pessimistic scenario. Given the various returns calculated from sensitivity analysis, those returns can be weighted by the probabilities accordingly, as shown in Table 6.5.

What can be seen from this calculation is that the "expected value" from the project is 11.4 percent. While this again may be useful information, it is not very realistic because 11.4 percent is not

**Table 6.5**

| Calculation of expected value | | | |
|---|---|---|---|
| *Scenario* | *Expected return %* | *Probabilty occurrence %* | *Weighted expected return* |
| Optimistic | 18 | 10 | 1.8 |
| Most likely | 13 | 60 | 7.8 |
| Pessimistic | 6 | 30 | 1.8 |
| Total weighted expected return (expected value) | | | 11.4 |

actually one of the returns that we expect. The most likely result is that we expect a return of 13 percent. Thus 11.4 percent is simply the average of various probabilities and they in turn have been based upon a subjective assessment of the likelihood of various outcomes by managers themselves. The approach is not very scientific!

The method described above uses probability estimates associated with the scenarios. Sensitivity analysis or a simulated model could also have probabilities assigned to them. Attaching probabilities to the various variables could be carried out in order to establish the most likely return given the probabilities of all the various sensitivities. Again we have to say that while this is possible we are not at all convinced that it actually helps in the decision-making process, because a sense of spurious accuracy is given to the calculations. On balance we feel that it is best to give sound, well-argued figures for the most likely scenario and leave it to managers to assess – probably subjectively – the likely variation in returns. This process will be discussed in Chapter 8.

# RISK MANAGEMENT

Risk in business has many faces. In the context of the strategic decision, we are not considering insurable risk – the possibility of fire or theft or other damaging event, but rather the risk that the results we expect do not happen – for whatever reason – and that firm fails to prosper as planned.

Some firms (or rather managers) are risk averse and will shun any move where there is even a tiny probability of less than desired results occurring. But for most, there is the old adage of "nothing ventured, nothing gained." However, most prudent managers (and investors, too) will try to minimize commercial risk by asking the question: If the worst possible outcome occurs will we, as a company, be able to survive, or will it kill us?

> **Risk management has many faces. In the context of the strategic decision, we are not considering insurable risk – the possibility of fire or theft or other damaging event, but rather the risk that the results we expect do not happen.**

So-called financial risk refers specifically to the level of debt in a company as opposed to equity capital and most firms have very precise limits on the amount of borrowing that is permitted – irrespective of the likely returns on the investment – because the "downside" in terms of what might happen to net income is too severe a penalty.

With ordinary commercial risk, we saw in Chapter 3 that diversification is a useful counter to a particular business foundering and the risk in many aspects of a firm's operations can be offset by keeping options open. For example, it may be more profitable to obtain materials from a single source, but if that source is stronger than the buyer, the risk is that they can hold you to ransom over those prices in the long run. Having two suppliers is suboptimal, but reduces the downside risk.

## You cannot have a super return with no risk

Risk, taken in the context of financial appraisal, is defined in a very specific manner: it expresses the degree of expected variation in the return of an investment. Mathematically this can be expressed in terms of the standard deviation of returns. However, the degree of sophistication in these calculations provides a false sense of security. It is possible to feel that all aspects of the possible returns have thus been considered and that the eventual return cannot possibly fall outside the range that has been forecast. The risk computations themselves, however, have been based upon future expectations and can therefore only be as reliable as those forecasts are reliable. The returns from the project could be even higher than was ever thought possible; alternatively the project could be a complete disaster and all your money could be lost.

However the major problem with all this risk analysis is as follows: The most likely return forecast for the project is very likely to be quite close to the rate of return required by managers (based on the weighted cost of capital calculation – see Chapter 7). The anticipated returns from projects are quite likely to cluster around, say, 15 percent and this may very well be the rate of return required by business managers. If this is the case all that risk analysis is likely to add to the decision-taking process is that, if all goes well, the project will achieve more than 15 percent and that, if all goes badly, the project will not achieve 15 percent! Although it may appear useful to have an awareness of the full range of possibilities – which risk assessment provides – how this additional information is actually taken into account in the final decision-making in practice will vary from company to company – and indeed from manager to manager.

# WIDER ISSUES

Of course it may be the case that other benefits were expected from the project. These are the so-called synergies with the rest of the organization which may be more or less than were originally expected. We shall discuss these issues at greater length in Chapter 9 when we consider the strategic fit of a particular investment proposal with the whole organization. But the effect of whether or not these synergies are achieved should perhaps be mentioned here, when discussing optimistic and pessimistic scenarios. The kinds of added benefits that a project might bring to a company, which may or may not be achieved, are:

- More economic production runs for all products following the introduction of the new product.

- A general reduction in overhead cost because of the spreading of general overhead or burden across a greater number of units.

- Additional sales for other products which follow the marketing of the new product.

- Knowledge, know-how and experience gained from producing a new product which may be important for research and development of new products in the future.

These positive synergies may or may not be achieved and they will affect the overall returns including the best and worse cases from the project. It is possible of course, that adding a new product line might have negative effects to the rest of the company:

- The introduction of new products may mean a reduction in sales of older, less technologically advanced products that the company is presently selling.

- New factories, new marketing and new sales forces may mean that overheads increase rather than decrease proportionately in the short run.

- Very large projects which are unsuccessful may mean that the whole company becomes financially unstable.

# APPENDIX: THE STANDARD DEVIATION

The most widely accepted measure of risk in finance puts a calculated value on the degree of variation that can be expected between budgeted and actual results. This means that, rather than simply saying that we are uncertain about the future cash flows from the investment, we can quantify the degree of risk by calculating a standard deviation of the expected return. We can say that if the most likely return (the mean) is 10 percent and the standard deviation is 5 percent, then there is a 95 percent chance that the actual return achieved from the investment will be between 20 percent and nil. (This does make the assumption that the expected returns are normally distributed).

The standard deviation of the expected rate of return of an investment can be calculated by making changes in the cash flow forecasts. Let us assume that estimates have been made that the return on the security card investment proposed as the basis for Table 6.1 in this chapter could lie between 0 percent and 20 percent. (This range of returns with their associated probabilities approximates to a normal distribution). Furthermore, when probabilities for the various returns are associated with each of them, the following result is obtained:

| Return expected % | Probability of occurrence % |
|---|---|
| 0 | 10 |
| 5 | 20 |
| 10 | 40 |
| 15 | 20 |
| 20 | 10 |

The expected value of the return for this project is 10 percent. The standard deviation may be calculated following the following steps:

---

**Standard deviation**
- Step 1: calculate the average return by adding up the returns weighted by their probability.
- Step 2: take away each individual return from the average return calculated in step 1 to obtain a difference figure.
- Step 3: square each difference figure in decimal format.
- Step 4: weight the squared differences by the probabilities and calculate the square root of the sum of those differences.

---

Table A1 shows how this process might be carried out for the proposed investment in security card equipment.

**Table A.1**

| Calculation of the standard deviation | | | | | |
|---|---|---|---|---|---|
| A | B | C | D | E | F |
| Expected return | Probability of occurrence | Weighted return $A \times B$ | Difference from average $C - A$ | Difference squared $D^2$ | Weighted difference squared $E \times B$ |
| % | % | % | % | | |
| 0 | 10 | 0 | 10 | 0.0100 | 0.0010 |
| 5 | 20 | 1 | 5 | 0.0025 | 0.0005 |
| 10 | 40 | 4 | 0 | 0 | 0 |
| 15 | 20 | 3 | −5 | 0.0025 | 0.0005 |
| 20 | 10 | 2 | −10 | 0.0100 | 0.0010 |
| | | 10 | | | 0.0030 |

Note: Standard deviation is the square root of 0.0030 = 0.0548 (that is 5.48%)

If we assume that the distribution of possible returns is normally distributed about the average return, the special feature of the standard deviation measure is that we can say:

- There is a 66.7 percent chance that actual results will fall within 1 standard deviation either side of the expected result.
- There is a 95 percent chance that actual results will fall within 2 standard deviations either side of the expected result.

The probability distribution assumed in the security card equipment project *approximates* to a normal distribution, so we can say that there is a 66.7 percent chance that the return on the project will be between 4.52 percent and 15.48 percent (10 percent ± 5.48 percent). There is a 95 percent chance that the project will achieve a return between − 0.96 percent and 20.96 percent (10 percent ± 2 × 5.48 percent). However, we would return you to the discussion in the chapter: How much value is this information when you are trying to decide whether or not to adopt a project which is to achieve a required rate of return? That rate of return sought, too, will almost certainly be between 0 percent and 20 percent!

What is crucial to this process is
the determination of the
required rate of return. It is
fundamental to the investment
decision-making process.

# Chapter 7

◆

# WHAT RATE OF RETURN SHOULD WE LOOK FOR?

The basic ground rules for an investment decision are founded on sound estimation of cash flows together with some estimation of the likely variation in those cash flows that may possibly take place in the actual event. Once forecast, the decision has to be taken as to whether or not the cash flows apparently give an adequate return. As we have seen the most sophisticated process for evaluating the cash flows from a

> **Once forecast, the decision has to be taken as to whether or not the cash flows apparently give an adequate return.**

financial point of view is a discounting process which provides a comparison for all the cash flows in present value terms. The variations in cash flows are taken account of by making an effort to measure risk in a variety of ways – using scenarios, sensitivity analysis or simulation techniques.

The discounting process takes either of two forms: net present value (NPV) or internal rate of return (IRR).

- NPV discounts the cash flows at a *required rate of return*, to see whether or not that rate of return is achieved by the investment. If the net present value is positive (or zero), then the required rate of return can be said to have been achieved.
- The IRR method finds the rate of return that is expected from the investment. In this case, if the IRR is greater than (or at least equal to) the *required rate of return*, the investment is acceptable.

Furthermore, if the analysis of risk indicates that the variation in the return expected from the investment is anticipated to be high, then managers may look for a higher *required rate of return*. This is because they will seek a premium for taking extra risk in an investment which has more likelihood that actual results could be very much different from the most likely expected results.

What is crucial in this process is the determination of the *required rate of return*. It is fundamental to the investment decision-making process and is the subject matter of this chapter.

# THE REQUIRED RATE OF RETURN

The required rate of return is a very sensitive figure: in other words very small changes in it have major implications in the decision-making process. The problem is that the difference between what is actually achieved and what is expected may be very small. If we could promise you a return of 11 percent on a particular investment you may very well accept it, but if we were to offer you a return of only 10 percent you may very well reject it. The difference does not seem to be very much but just think how much more you would be pleased with 1 percent per year increase in your wages, or in your pension, or on your savings. Such differences in finance are very small but could make all the difference.

So the rate of discount used or the rate of return required is a most important factor in determining whether or not to undertake the investment and the difference between accepting the investment or rejecting it may be very small. This means that, ideally, it is neces-

128

sary to establish the rate of return required with some degree of accuracy.

What rate of return should we be looking for from an investment? So much effort has been given to finding exactly what the discount rate should be. Volumes have been written about the calculation of the rate of interest required from an investment. What all the theory boils down to is this:

> **What basically matters to investors is the return they expect to receive from their investment taking into account the risk involved.**

The return they require, as we shall see, is based upon what return they expect they can achieve from similar, alternative investments, the level of interest rates in general, and expectations about the levels of inflation and growth in the economy as a whole. The risk that they take on board is the possibility that they may not achieve the rate of return they require, although that is counterbalanced by the fact that you might do better than expected. Thus, the return that investors want, or expect, or require is made up of two elements – a fundamental return and a premium for risk:

1 **A fundamental return for making an investment.** When an investment is made, capital is being given up now in the expectation of a return later. We have seen how this translates into cash flows: by giving up cash flow now (rather than enjoying the benefits that the cash can buy now) there is the expectation of gaining more cash flow.

2 **A premium for risk taking.** Risk is measured by calculating the variability of the returns expected from the investment. The risk premium is the potential extra return sought because of the uncertainty – that you might not get exactly the return you require from the investment. In principle, the more risk the more risk premium sought.

There are, in fact, two kinds of investor in a company: the shareholders of the company and the lenders to it. The major differences between these two are:

129

- Shareholders "own" the company and theoretically control what the company does. Lenders to the company have no such rights (although they may indirectly influence how the company carries on its business!)

- Shareholders do not have to be given an annual cash payment as a return for their investment. Lenders certainly do expect such a return by way of interest on the money they have lent to the company[1].

Both these groups of investors expect a return which takes into account some allowance for risk. We shall now look at how the returns required by shareholders, on the one hand, and by lenders, on the other, are established in practice.

# THE RETURN TO SHAREHOLDERS

A major reason for investing in shares on the stockmarket is that there is an expectation of higher returns than that which would be received from an investment in government securities. For example, while an investor in government stocks might only expect to receive 4–5 percent, that same investor might expect to achieve 10–12 percent by investing in shares on a stock exchange. The extra return is the so-called risk premium. The investor expects to receive this extra return because the value of shares can go down as well as up. The higher return is expected for taking this risk.

The return that shareholders actually receive when they invest in the shares of a company is achieved in two parts: a dividend receipt and a growth in the share price. Shareholders expect to receive a dividend of between 2 percent and 5 percent of the market value of the share in the UK and the USA (less in Japan). So if a share is currently priced at 280p on the UK stockmarket, holders of that share will expect to receive around 10p per year as a dividend. As this is not a very high return – and certainly not enough to compensate for the risk involved in a stockmarket investment – the shareholder

[1] It is possible to have "zero coupon" loans which pay no annual interest – just a premium when the capital is repaid.

will expect some extra return on the investment. This comes by way of an increase in the share price – that is, growth in the value of the investment.

The fact that companies grow is inherent in stockmarket invest-ment. Shareholders expect the com-pany they have invested in to grow over time. This is now such a strong belief and one that has been con-firmed over very many years in many stockmarkets that investors in equity (shareholding) *expect* that the value of their shares will grow.

**The fact that companies grow is inherent in stock-market investment. Shareholders expect the company they have invested in to grow over time.**

Where does share capital growth come from? Why should the value of a firm's shares increase over time? The answer is that strategically speaking companies either grow or they die. It is diffi-cult for them to stand still. As we discussed in Chapter 1, companies need to make capital investment to support their strategies, and this investment makes them larger – they grow in size. The dynamics, from an accounting point of view, are that a company does not dis-tribute all its profits by way of a dividend. Some profits are retained and it is those funds which are ploughed back into the business. New assets are bought with the funds and the company's size grows accordingly. The larger sized the company is the greater its value, so the shareholders obtain growth in the price of their shares.

## The cost of equity

The return achieved by shareholders consists of a dividend and a growth in share price. Both of these can be expressed as an annual amount relative to the share price, so the percentage return to shareholders is:

annual dividend/share price (as %)          = dividend yield (A)
plus
growth in share price over one year/share price (as %)    = growth rate   (B)
Total annual percentage return                 = A + B

Table 7.1 shows a numerical example of all this.

**Table 7.1**

| Calculation of the cost of equity |
|---|

The price of AB plc's shares on the London stockmarket on January 1 were 250p. By December 31 of the same year they had risen to 290p. During the year dividends amounting to 10p were paid to the shareholders.

Dividend yield $\dfrac{10}{250} = 4\%$

Growth in share price as % of opening share price: $\dfrac{40}{250} = 16\%$

Total annual percentage return $\qquad\qquad\qquad\qquad\qquad 20\%$

From the company management's point of view this is an estimate of the return *required* by shareholders on any new investment and is thus regarded by them as being the "cost of equity" – the cost of using shareholders funds – for any new investment.

## Shareholders' return and risk

Neither part of the return is certain: the dividend nor the growth in the share price. The dividend may be cut and the expected increase in value of the share may not be forthcoming. As we discussed in Chapter 6, events may not happen as originally expected, so investments in the business may not pay off as expected. Such is the risk of investment in shares on a stock exchange. Only in exceptional circumstances will the dividend be less than expected. Senior management of companies try desperately to maintain the level of dividend. Because dividends are for the most part paid in cash, the markets tend to think that a company has a serious cash flow crisis if it is unable to maintain at least the same dividend as last year. A cut in share dividend will often have a dramatic effect on a share's price, though paying a dividend greater than the profits has the effect of shrinking the size of the company.

The greater risk to the return expected by a shareholder is in the level of growth in share price that is actually achieved. Dividends are rarely very different from one year to another, but growth rates differ greatly. Share prices can go down as well as up. The reason may be because of the specific activity of the company itself – either achieving much better or worse results from new investment (or of course from its ongoing business, where profits also may be increasing or decreasing more than expected).

Growth in profits may also vary because of the general economic climate or other factors which will affect all shares on a stock exchange. Such *systematic risk*, as it is called, will mean that expectations about changes in future profits will affect all shares and the feature of this is that all shares will tend to increase in value or decrease in value at the same time. Just notice what happens when a central bank announces an increase in interest rates. All share prices fall following such an announcement[2]. The reason is twofold: the lower share price provides a higher dividend yield to compensate for the higher return expected from government stocks (following the interest rate rise). Also higher interest rates will mean a higher cost of borrowing and higher required returns in general. Such higher required returns will mean that fewer investments can be found to achieve those returns – marginal projects will not be proceeded with. Consequently, the growth in share prices will be less, because of the lower amount of capital investment in the business. This will depress share prices on the stock market.

The major problem is assessing the level of risk that is involved. For example, is an investment in a printing firm more risky than opening up a fast-food restaurant? Is an investment in a coalmine more or less risky (from a financial point of view) than setting up a factory to produce computer chips? Even if we can say which is the more risky investment it is extremely difficult to say how much extra return should be expected from the more risky of the two investments. Say we expect the return from the restaurant to be more risky than the return from the printing firm. Would a return of 12 percent from the restaurant be enough to compensate the

---

[2] It is actually quite possible that shares generally have *anticipated* a rise in interest rates. In this case, the increase in interest rates by the government when it happens may cause shares to *rise* in value, because the increase in interest rates was not as much as expected!

extra risk, if a return of just 10 percent per year was expected from the printing firm? Essentially what we are saying here is: is the risk premium of 2 percent adequate to compensate for the extra risk of the investment in the restaurant?

## The capital asset pricing model

The classic theory, developed over thirty years ago, which attempts to answer this question is what is known as the capital asset pricing model (CAPM). The assumption in the CAPM is that the risk premium required from a particular investment may be calculated from stockmarket information.

The CAPM states that the risk premium associated with any particular investment will depend on whether the investment's returns are expected to vary by more or less than the average return on the market. If we remember that a shareholder obtains a return by way of a dividend and a growth in the share price, the variability of these two elements may be more or less than the average variability of dividends and growth rates of all shares in the market. In fact, the CAPM only takes the variability of growth rates into account. It does not consider comparative variations in dividends.

If a share's variability is expected to be 20 percent more than that of the market, the market risk premium will be multiplied by 1.2. If the variability of a particular share's growth rate is much the same as that of the market, the risk premium used to establish the return required from investments in the company will be the same as that of the market. That is, the market risk premium will be multiplied by 1.0.

Analysis of historical data can assess whether or not an investment is likely to vary more than the market. Growth rates are calculated by company share prices at two points in time. Therefore, volatility in growth rates is affected by the volatility of share prices. Consequently, the variation in share prices (up and down) is measured over a period of time in order to establish a measure of the variability of the return expected. Companies with high share price volatility tend to be in certain industries, whereas companies which have lower than average share price variability tend to be in other industries.

In the theory of the CAPM the return that shareholders expect from an investment is based upon a "fundamental" rate of return plus a premium for taking risk multiplied by an individual share's measure of variability:

| Return required by shareholders | = | Basic risk-free rate of return | + | Share's measure of variability | × | Market risk premium |
|---|---|---|---|---|---|---|

The fundamental rate of return may be assumed to be what one might expect from government securities – government bonds or gilts. This rate of return is regarded as being practically risk free. The risk premium required can be established using the general risk premium of the market as a whole. Putting numbers on these factors is extremely controversial. Some specialist financial advisers and analysts take the risk-free rate to be 8 percent in the UK; others take it to be 6 percent. The market risk premium has been calculated over very long periods as being anything between 6 percent and 10 percent. To some extent the actual numbers depend upon the anticipated rate of inflation in an economy and this is something that we deal with below.

The measure of the company's share variability compared to the market is known as its beta. This term comes from the mathematics of the CAPM (which was developed originally using Greek letters in the algebraic arguments). Table 7.2 shows how the cost of equity would be calculated using different betas for three companies. As most companies' betas fall within the range 0.8 to 1.2, Table 7.2 shows that most required equity returns in the UK will fall between 12.4 percent and 15.6 percent. This may seem a very narrow range within which equity returns may be expected to fall. There are two points that should be made about this:

1 We have said before that, in financial decision-taking, the difference between acceptance and rejection of a strategy may be very small – in terms of the return sought and the return expected to be achieved.

2 The CAPM provides a figure for the *cost* of equity – the rate of return required by a company. This is not the rate of return

**Table 7.2**

| **Examples of the cost of equity using CAPM** |
| --- |

Assume that:
  Risk free rate of return is 6%
  Market risk premium is 8%

For beta = 1.2

  Return on equity = 6% + 1.2 × 8% = 15.6%

For beta = 1.0

  Return on equity = 6% + 1.0 × 8% = 14%

For beta = 0.8

  Return on equity = 6% + 0.8 × 8% = 12.4%

achieved. Much higher returns may, in practice, be achieved than that which is required. These are the investments and strategies we are seeking.

What becomes quite apparent from this analysis is that whereas we need a particularly accurate figure for assessing the required rate of return from an investment, all the theory over the years has only produced controversial basic figures which give us a range of answers.

## Raising funds by borrowing

Of course some of the funds that are required to finance an investment may be borrowed from banks or other institutions. Borrowing can be raised at a known rate of interest. Even if it has not already been raised, a good estimate of the rate that will have to be paid for the borrowed money can be made. For example, if you are raising a mortgage on your house you will contact a number of banks and savings and loans companies or building societies to obtain quotations for their borrowing rates. This will give you a good idea of the market price for the borrowing – that is the cost of borrowing.

The cost of borrowing or "debt" is, strictly speaking, its "yield to maturity." This is the same as the internal rate of return on the debt and includes the consideration for repayment of the debt in a number of years' time. Simply, if you borrow £100 now and repay £100 in 5 years' time at 10 percent interest, then the yield to maturity is 10 percent. However, you might agree to pay the bank a premium of £5 on repayment of the debt in 5 years' time – so that you repay £105 in 5 years' time rather than £100. In this case the yield to maturity, or effective rate of interest paid on the debt, is 10.8 percent – slightly higher than the "coupon" rate of 10 percent. Table 7.3 sets out the calculations by showing that the internal rate of return of such a cash flow stream is 10.8 percent.

It is true that loans can be taken out with variable interest rates (or "floating rate" loans). Typically, mortgages raised in the UK for house purchase are of this kind. The rate of interest can be increased or decreased under the terms of the loan by the lender at any time. The yield to maturity calculation is a little more complex if rates vary over the life of the loan, but the principle of the calcula-

**Table 7.3**

| **Yield to maturity** | | |
|---|---|---|
| £100 borrowed now at 10% interest per year. | | |
| £105 to be repaid at the end of 5 years. | | |
| The cash flows paid out on the loan are discounted at 10.8% to achieve an NPV of zero. This means that the yield to maturity of the loan is 10.8% | | |
| | *Cash flows* | *Present value using 10.8% interest* |
| | £ | £ |
| Year 0 | +100 | 100 |
| Year 1 | −10 | −9 |
| Year 2 | −10 | −8 |
| Year 3 | −10 | −7 |
| Year 4 | −10 | −7 |
| Year 5 | −115* | −69 |
| Net present value | | 0 |

*£10 annual interest plus £105 repaid

tion is the same as that shown in Table 7.3. The major problem, at the point of taking up the loan, is to forecast the interest rate(s) that will actually be paid on the loan over the period of the loan.

# THE WEIGHTED AVERAGE COST OF CAPITAL

Some companies will have no borrowed money. They will have raised all their capital from their shareholders or from the profits they have ploughed back into the business. In this case the cost of capital for such companies is the cost of shareholders funds. No adjustment has to be made for the probably cheaper funds that may be obtained by borrowing.

Where the company has some funds which it has borrowed, as well as shareholders' funds, the costs of each of these two sources of finance have to be averaged out. The average is not a simple average but is weighted by the amount of capital raised from each source. If 60 percent of the funds are from shareholders then their cost of capital is weighted by 60 percent and the cost of borrowing by 40 percent. The formula for the weighted cost of capital is set out as follows:

| Weighted average cost of capital | = | Proportion of shareholders' funds | × | Cost of equity | + | Proportion of borrowed funds | × | Cost of debt |
|---|---|---|---|---|---|---|---|---|

The proportion of shareholders funds to borrowing is established in either one of two methods. The proportions, or weights, may be based on:

- the book value of the shareholders funds and borrowing; or
- the market value of each.

There are arguments for and against using either book values or market values of the debt and equity. Some analysts use book values because these change only periodically, for example, when profits are made and shareholders' funds are increased or when repayments of debt are made and that reduces the amount borrowed. Others feel it is more realistic to use market values because they more accurately indicate the proper weight of funds drawn from each source of capital. The trouble with market values is that, particularly for shares, prices go down as well as up. Consequently the value of equity and therefore the weight given to equity will alter as general stockmarket conditions change. The average cost of capital goes down (less weight given to the cost of equity) when the price of shares fall on the market – and vice versa when the value of shares increases.

Table 7.4 sets out the calculation of the weighted average cost of capital for a small company called Commerce Inc. The table shows:

- A simplified balance sheet of the US-based company.
- How the weights for the weighted average cost of capital calculation would be established.
- The calculation of the weighted average cost of capital – given that the cost of shareholders' funds is 15.2 percent and the cost of debt is 9.8 percent.

It must be remembered that the expected return from a particular investment is likely to be close to the cost of capital. Therefore it is necessary to be fairly precise about the average cost of capital. This lengthy debate about exactly what is the cost of equity, the cost of debt, and the weights to be used to calculate the weighted average cost of capital suggests, however, a good deal of uncertainty about exactly what rate of return we are seeking from a particular investment. The discussion about risk in Chapter 6 indicated that we will almost certainly be uncertain about what the actual return from the investment will be. What we are suggesting in this chapter is that there is some doubt as to exactly what is the return we require from the investment. We are about to add two further considerations to this already complicated process: inflation and taxation. Their effects upon the weighted average cost of capital complicate matters even more.

# WHAT SHOULD BE DONE ABOUT INFLATION?

Generally speaking, what will happen if we take inflation into account when estimating the cash flows expected from an invest-

**Table 7.4**

## The calculation of the weighted average cost of capital

*Balance Sheet of Commerce Inc as at December 31st*

| Assets | $m |
|---|---|
| Current assets | 41.0 |
| Property, plant and equipment | 56.7 |
| | $97.7 |

| Liabilities and Share-Owners' Equity | |
|---|---|
| Current | 32.0 |
| Long-term debt | 16.2 |
| Share-owners' equity | |
|    Common stock, 13.3m $1 shares issued | 13.3 |
|    Capital surplus | 15.1 |
|    Reinvested earnings | 21.1 |
| | 49.5 |
| | $97.7 |

| *Weights based on book values:* | $m | % |
|---|---|---|
| Share-owners' equity | 49.5 | 75.3 |
| Borrowing/debt | 16.2 | 24.7 |
| Total | 65.7 | 100.0 |

| *Weights based on market values:* | $m | % |
|---|---|---|
| The market value of share-owners' equity, assuming current share price is $6.03 per share, is: | | |
|    13.3m shares × $6.03 | 80.2 | 83.2 |
| The market value of the borrowing is assumed to be its nominal value | 16.2 | 16.8 |
| Total | 94.4 | 100.0 |

*The weighted cost of capital*
Assuming,
   (1) Cost of share-owners' equity is 15.2% and (2) the cost of borrowing is 9.8% then the weighed average cost of capital is:

**Based on book values:**
   75.3% × 15.2% + 24.7% × 9.8% = 13.8%

**Based on market values:**
   83.2% × 15.2% + 16.8% × 9.8% = 14.3%

ment is that all the cash flows will be greater. This does not mean that the investment will be any better – just that the numbers will be higher. Think of your expenses claim month by month. If there is inflation and your travelling or car expenses increase, you simply claim more cash. You don't feel any better off, because the cash you claim back is simply the amount that you spend.

If inflation is taken into account in the investment appraisal process, its effect on all the factors which go into making up cash flow is anticipated. The cash flows so obtained will be in *nominal* or monetary terms. If consideration of inflation is excluded from the cash flow forecast, then the investment is being considered in *real* terms. In this case, the cash flows generated will be estimated under the assumption that prices and costs will remain the same – at least as far as inflation is concerned. Again, taking the example of an expenses claim: You may budget for your travelling expenses each month next year at constant prices – say, £2,000 per month; or you may estimate that inflation will increase those costs at a rate of, say, 3 percent *per year* – so that the expenses will increase from £2,000 in month 1 to £2,005 in month 2 and so on. What you actually do will depend on the management accounting procedures in your particular organization.

The same is the case in capital budgeting. Cash flow forecasts may be prepared for investment appraisal in nominal terms or in real terms. Whichever method is used should be laid down in the firm's management accounting procedures. Some firms ignore inflation and prepare all cash flow forecasts on the basis of constant prices. This is certainly the case in many government agencies which are looking to provide a service in the most economic way. An example in the UK would be an investment decision in a National Health hospital where it was being considered whether or not to purchase an expensive piece of capital equipment, for example a scanner. Others argue that thinking in nominal terms is easier and more realistic, because, they argue, we automatically take inflation into account when making estimates of monetary figures into the future. So, in this case, revenues and costs will be initially considered at today's prices and then inflated by the rate that it is expected inflation will affect those prices.

When it comes to investment decisions, then, inflation simply *adds* to the amount of the cash flow. The cash flows will be higher than they would be otherwise – as shown in the example in Table 7.5.

**Table 7.5**

### An example of how inflation simply increases the cash flow numbers

Superstores make the following estimates of revenues and cash costs at their proposed new store over the next five years:

| Based on constant prices (£000s) | Year 1 £ | Year 2 £ | Year 3 £ | Year 4 £ | Year 5 £ |
|---|---|---|---|---|---|
| Sales revenue | 3,015 | 3,261 | 3,117 | 2,996 | 2,870 |
| Cost of goods sold | 2,436 | 2,602 | 2,478 | 2,394 | 2,293 |
| | 579 | 659 | 639 | 602 | 577 |
| Store expenses (excl. depreciation) | 407 | 425 | 454 | 431 | 398 |
| Cash generated | 172 | 234 | 185 | 171 | 179 |
| *Allowing for 3.5% inflation (£000s)* | | | | | |
| Sales revenue | 3,121 | 3,493 | 3,455 | 3,438 | 3,409 |
| Cost of goods sold | 2,521 | 2,787 | 2,747 | 2,747 | 2,723 |
| | 599 | 706 | 708 | 691 | 686 |
| Store expenses (excl. depreciation) | 421 | 455 | 503 | 495 | 473 |
| Cash generated | 178 | 251 | 205 | 196 | 213 |

## Inflation and the required rate of return

As the cash flows are higher because of the effect of inflation on the estimated cash flows, then it is reasonable for the investor to require a higher rate of return from the investment. Why? If inflation generally is expected to be 10 percent, investors will require a return of 6 percent more than if the level of inflation is expected to be only 4 percent. The reason for this is so that the original capital is recovered and *maintains its value* in real terms. Table 7.6 presents a numerical example of this.

## Adjusting the discount rate

What amount of adjustment to the required rate of return is needed in the decision-making process? In finance the discount rate used to

## Table 7.6

### Maintaining the value of capital intact

A company can make an investment of £1,000 with returns over 3 years of £402 per year at constant prices. The investment is fully depreciating – nothing is left at the end of 3 years – and the company is looking for a return (in real terms) of 10%. As the calculation below shows, providing £302 is put aside and reinvested at 10%, then the company will have a cash deposit of £1,000 at the end of the 3 years – and it will have earned 10% per year from the investment of £1,000.

| | Cash flow | Income (return) | Capital put aside | Interest on capital (10% cumulative) Year 2 | Year 3 | Total capital accumulated |
|---|---|---|---|---|---|---|
| | £ | £ | £ | £ | £ | £ |
| Year 0 | −1,000 | | | | | |
| 1 | 402 | 100 | 302 | 30 | 34 | 366 |
| 2 | 402 | 100 | 302 | – | 30 | 332 |
| 3 | 402 | 100 | 302 | – | – | 302 |

Capital put aside plus accumulated interest equals original capital £1,000

If there was inflation of 5% per year, the cash flows generated from the same investment could be expected to be 5% more each year: that is £422, £443 and £465 for the 3 years. If 5% more capital was put aside and it earned interest adequate to compensate for inflation, sufficient capital would be accumulated to be equivalent, in nominal terms, to the £1,000 originally invested.

The interest the annual deposits would have to earn would be approximately 10% (required) plus 5% (inflation) which equals 15%. Strictly speaking, the interest earned has to be 15.5% – obtained from the following calculation (a multiplication of rates rather than a sum):

$$100 \times (1 + 0.10) \times (1 + 0.05) - 100 = 15.5$$

In order to maintain the capital value (its "earning power") of the original £1,000, the amount of capital in 3 years' time would have to be £1,158, that is £1,000 inflated at 5% for 3 years. That is what is achieved if the cash flows generated from the investment are £422, £443 and £465 over the 3 years:

| | Cash flow | Income (return) | Capital put aside | Interest on capital (10% cumulative) Year 2 | Year 3 | Total capital accumulated |
|---|---|---|---|---|---|---|
| | £ | £ | £ | £ | £ | £ |
| Year 0 | −1,000 | | | | | |
| 1 | 422 | 105 | 317 | 39 | 57 | 423 |
| 2 | 443 | 110 | 333 | – | 52 | 385 |
| 3 | 465 | 116 | – | – | – | 350 |

Accumulated capital sum equivalent to £1,000 inflated at 5% for 3 years £1,158 calculate the present value of nominal cash flows (those increased by expected levels of inflation) is also increased by the general rate of inflation.

It is all a question of comparing like with like. If no account is taken of inflation then the proper thing to do is to expect a real rate of interest to be achieved by the investment. If inflation is taken into account – and we are dealing with nominal cash flows – then the thing to do is to expect a nominal or monetary market rate of interest from the investment. The rates of return that companies should seek to achieve on any new investment is based upon the weighted average cost of capital as explained earlier. That WACC takes account of the appropriate level of risk of the investment in the cost of shareholders' funds, within this calculation. It almost certainly takes account of the *expected* level of inflation in the economy. The risk-free rate which is part of the calculation of shareholders' cost of capital and the interest rate required by lenders will both be affected by the anticipated levels of inflation in general. So the costs of capital that have been used earlier to calculate the WACC were in nominal terms – the costs allowed for inflation. If that WACC is used then, we must make sure that we are discounting cash flows which are also in nominal terms – that is, the effect of inflation has been built into their calculation as well.

Table 7.7 shows a numerical example based on the example in Table 7.5 which indicates the fact that theoretically the same decision should be arrived at whether or not inflation is taken into account. However, we would advise taking inflation into account because of the differential effects inflation may have upon the cash flows expected from the investment.

## Differential inflation

Say wages are increasing at 5 percent and there is a 3 percent general increase in the level of prices. An important consideration in such a situation is whether the extra wages cost can be passed on in a proportionate increase in sales prices to customers. Consideration of the different level of inflation of the various estimates of sales revenues and costs making up the overall cash flow from invest-

**Table 7.7**

---

### Comparing like with like

- Discounting real cash flows at the real rate of interest
- Discounting nominal cash flows at the nominal rate of interest

In Table 7.5 the cash flows of a project over 5 years based on constant prices and costs on the one hand and inflated prices and costs on the other were as follows:

|  | Year 1 | Year 2 | Year 3 | Year 4 | Year 5 |
|---|---|---|---|---|---|
| **Based on constant prices (£000s)** | | | | | |
| Cash generated | 172 | 234 | 185 | 171 | 179 |
| **Allowing for 3.5% inflation (£000s)** | | | | | |
| Cash generated | 178 | 251 | 205 | 196 | 213 |

If the cash flows generated on constant prices, are discounted at the real rate of return – say 13% and the cash flows generated allowing for inflation of 3.5% are discounted at the nominal rate of return – 16.955%* – the present value of each of the cash flows will be:

|  | Year 1 | Year 2 | Year 3 | Year 4 | Year 5 |
|---|---|---|---|---|---|
| **Based on constant prices (£000s)** | | | | | |
| Cash generated | 172 | 234 | 185 | 171 | 179 |
| Discounted at 13% | 152 | 183 | 128 | 105 | 97 |
| **Allowing for 3.5% inflation (£000s)** | | | | | |
| Cash generated | 178 | 251 | 205 | 196 | 213 |
| Discounted at 16.955% | 152 | 183 | 128 | 105 | 97 |

Thus the total present value of each of these cash flow streams is the same – and totals £665,000

---

*Calculated as illustrated in Table 7.6 as: $100 \times (1 + 0.13) \times (1 + 0.035) - 100 = 16.955$

ment will highlight the difficulties of the effects of inflation upon the investment decision. Thinking in real terms – simply assuming that prices will remain unchanged over the life of the investment – assumes that there are no differential rates of inflation expected in the future.

Sometimes it is difficult to distinguish price changes from cyclical effects. For example, the worldwide price of aluminum follows

THE STRATEGIC INVESTMENT DECISION

a cycle where prices go down as well as up. This depends upon the demand and supply situation in the aluminum production market. When prices are on the way up, it is difficult to say how much is due to inflation and how much is due to the pressure on prices because of excess demand for aluminum. For this reason it is probably best simply to look at the expected costs of such a material as aluminum over the life of an investment which uses aluminum as a raw material, taking into account likely price increases and decreases. Thinking in terms of real prices in such a market makes the calculations very convoluted.

It is therefore advisable to use differential rates of inflation. This means looking at each element of the cash flow calculations and seeking to show the effect of likely levels of inflation upon each type of revenue or cost. The main thing to remember is to compare like with like:

- If a consideration of inflation has been included then it is important to compare the investment with a market rate of return.

- If the cash flow forecast has been carried out at constant prices then all the investor should be looking for is a real rate of return.

## TAXATION AND OTHER FISCAL INCENTIVES

Wherever a strategic investment decision is being contemplated, it has to be emphasized that tax will undoubtedly affect the decision. It is beyond the scope of this book either to outline exactly how tax should be taken into account in cash flow computations or to explain how calculations should be undertaken, but it is vital that tax is included in any calculations about an investment proposal. It just makes a difference. It is not only the amount of tax paid which makes a difference. It is the incidence of tax – when it is paid – and

> **Wherever a strategic investment decision is being contemplated, it has to be emphasized that tax will undoubtedly affect the decision.**

allowances that are given for tax purposes for capital investment which will have an effect on the cash flows.

It may well be that the inclusion of tax may mean that the decision will be taken to undertake the investment rather than not. It may be that tax has a positive effect, ironically, because of the allowances given by the tax authorities. In this sense tax may be a good thing, although we all would like to pay less. So always make sure that someone calculates the taxation effects on the investment. This will be particularly important if you are making an investment abroad in a country where you are not familiar with the tax regulations. In that case you may have to take local financial advice in order to calculate the effects of taxation on the cash flows expected from the investment. Shell and Siemens' decisions will have been significantly influenced by tax and other governmental inducements, as indeed was Euro Disney.

Table 7.8 shows an investment proposal in the UK which has a negative net present value before taxation is taken into account, but which has a positive net present value when the effects of taxation are included.

The example in Table 7.8 as in all capital investment decisions relies very much on a *post tax* expected rate of return. The complications of establishing a *post tax* discount rate, just add a further level of complexity to the financial decision-making process.

## Differing stock (inventory) valuation methods

The various accounting techniques which value the stock or inventory at the balance sheet date will create different profit figures, but will not affect cash flow. Stocks or inventories can be valued on the basis of first-in-first-out (FIFO) or last-in-first-out (LIFO) – or even some averaging method. Profits will be affected by the valuation method and thus the tax payable. (In some countries, like the UK, the tax authorities legislate for a particular stock valuation method which has to be used for tax purposes – for calculating the amount of profit that will be taken).

Although stock valuation methods affect profits, they do not affect cash flows – directly. However, if more or less tax is *paid*, the cash flows from an investment will be changed.

**Table 7.8**

### The impact of taxation on capital investment proposals

A capital investment of £20m in plant and machinery which will have an economic life of 5 years has the expected pre-tax cash flows shown in the figures below. In the UK, depreciation allowances against tax amount to 25% per year on such assets, but on a reducing balance, so the allowance gets smaller and smaller each year – as shown. The taxable income consists of the pre-tax cash flow generated by the project less the allowances for the capital investment. Such taxable income is taxed at 33% in the UK and the tax is paid (or recovered) in the following year.

The pre-tax cash flows discounted at the pre-tax cost of capital (assumed to be 13% here) show a negative net present value. The post-tax cash flows discounted at the post-tax cost of capital provide a *positive* net present value. The post tax cost of capital is taken to be:

$$13\% \times (1 - 0.33) = 8.71\%$$

|  | Pre-tax cash flows £ | Capital allowances £ | Taxable income £ | Tax payable £ | Post-tax cash flows £ |
|---|---|---|---|---|---|
| Capital investment | -20,000 |  |  |  | -20,000 |
| Year 1 | 1,000 | 5,000 | -4,000 |  | 1,000 |
| Year 2 | 4,400 | 3,750 | 650 | -1,320 | 5,720 |
| Year 3 | 9,280 | 2,813 | 6,467 | 214 | 9,066 |
| Year 4 | 5,800 | 2,109 | 3,691 | 2,134 | 3,666 |
| Year 5 | 5,500 | 1,582 | 3,918 | 1,218 | 4,282 |
| Sale of plant   Year 5 | 4,746 |  |  | 1,293 | 3,453 |
| Net present value | -£368 |  |  |  | +£325 |

# CONCLUSION

In this chapter, we have identified a growing complexity in the ability to define the "correct" *required rate of return* from an investment. The difficulties involve dealing satisfactorily with:

- the cost of equity
  - the basic return
  - the premium for taking risk
- the cost of debt
- the weighted average cost of capital
- the impact of inflation

- the impact of tax
- post-tax discount rates

After all this – there are no really satisfactory answers as to what the appropriate discount rate should be or what is the "correct" cost of capital. So how are we to know whether or not to proceed with the investment when we are discounting cash flows about which we are uncertain with a rate of return about which we are also uncertain?

The issue can probably best be resolved by answering some seemingly simple questions:

1 What discount rate (other things being equal and with a high degree of certainty) will assist the company to achieve its corporate objective(s)?

2 If our aim is to double the value of shareholders' investment over five years, what rate of return achieves this?

3 Even if we build in a worst case scenario are the risks worthwhile?

4 If the investment passes the rate of return test, does the investment make strategic sense overall?

It is to the answer of this last question that we now turn.

◆

"Great manufacturing strategies are built on unique skills and capabilities, not on investments in buildings, equipment or specific individuals."

(Hayes and Pisano, "Beyond World-Class: The New Manufacturing Strategy," Harvard Business Review, January/February 1994)

◆

# Chapter 8

◆

# WHAT ELSE NEEDS TO BE TAKEN INTO ACCOUNT?

What we have been dealing with in the last few chapters are the techniques used in the financial appraisal of long-term capital investment proposals. We have outlined how the numbers for such investment appraisals are obtained and suggested that many of these are based upon estimates and forecasts of the future. If the degree of risk involved in the project is to be included in the evaluation, some assessment will have to be made as to how near to those forecasts we expect the actual outcome to be. A risky project is one where it is thought that the eventual results may stray widely from the original forecasts. A safe project is one where actual results are expected to be quite close to original estimates. All this information needs to be evaluated and assessed before a decision can be made. What should be clear by now is that the financial figures and analysis do not make the decision for us. At the end of the day, it will be the managers who are making the investment decision, who will weigh up all the information available, and take the decision that they feel happiest with accordingly.

> At the end of the day, it will be the managers who are making the investment decision, who will weigh up all the information available, and take the decision that they feel happiest with accordingly.

What this means is that managers use their experience to take the decision based upon all the information that they have available. Much academic research has been carried out asking invest-

ment managers which techniques they use when making investment decisions. It has shown that business managers use, to a
greater or lesser degree, each of the financial techniques we have
discussed in earlier chapters. But where managers have been
given an opportunity to say whether they use management judgment when making investment decisions as well as the financial
techniques, it has always been found that the use of management
judgment has been more important than any one of the techniques of investment appraisal.

There are good reasons for this. Financial appraisal only points
in a particular direction – it gives an idea of the *expected* return
and the associated risk of the proposal, but it may not incorporate
the whole picture. The numbers alone cannot encapsulate all that
there is in making a strategic investment decision. Projects can
rarely be taken in isolation. In fact the whole rationale of this
book is that investment decisions should be taken in their strategic context. It is rare that financial appraisal will encapsulate all
the ramifications of an investment proposal.

# MANAGEMENT JUDGMENT

Sometimes the situation arises where managers have been faced with an internal rate of return on a project of, say, only 5 percent but where they "feel" that the project is worth pursuing. Because the required rate of return is higher than 5 percent, the net present value (NPV) will be negative and taking on the investment will appear to reduce wealth, but even so a number of managers feel the project should go ahead. They will have the wider implications from the introduction of the project in mind when they argue their point. Comments such as the following are made to justify the project:

*"We have to be in this emerging market in order to protect our position or maintain our share in the marketplace."*

*"This new product will open up a whole new market segment."*

*"The introduction of a new product will motivate staff and encourage customers to see us in a progressive light."*

*"The innovation introduced by the capital investment will have an impact upon our development for years to come."*

*"If we don't do it, one of our competitors will."*

**"If we don't do it, one of our competitors will."**

Comments such as these relate to the qualitative aspects of the project – or at least to those issues which are difficult to measure. What is clear in such cases is that the financial figures – particularly taking the investment in isolation – do not take into account the somewhat more intangible (or, at best, unquantifiable) elements of the decision.

# PROJECTS CANNOT BE TAKEN IN ISOLATION

Strategic decisions cannot be made in isolation. They have to form part of the overall strategic fit. Any single investment will therefore be one of a series of investments over time which may or may not be planned from the outset. Euro Disney's prospectus in 1989 outlined a Phase I development which was evaluated over twenty-five years! At the same time, a Phase II to open in 1996 was also envisaged and appraised over 25 years. This example of planning was very forward looking and perhaps quite rare. The period of future strategic planning, as we have made clear earlier, very much depends upon the industry concerned: the oil industry will have a much longer planning horizon than the computer industry. But each investment decision should ideally be taken as one in a continuum – one in a whole series of investments.

**Each investment decision should ideally be taken as one in a continuum – one in a whole series of investments.**

Furthermore, a specific investment in capital assets – plant, equipment, and similar facilities – cannot readily be separated from a whole series of such investments and in what might be termed "human capital." The people in the firm will develop their skills and expertise and knowledge over time. The value of the development of this human capital will also increase as the organization grows. The improvement in people skills will carry over from one investment to another and the cost and benefits of such development cannot easily be tied to one investment rather than another.

Perhaps one way of establishing the value of the intangible aspects of a decision, is to consider the cost of *not* investing in a particular project. Usually, when projects are considered, the status quo is assumed if the project is not undertaken. But this can rarely be the case. See the example of James plc below. The decision not to undertake the new investment is saying so much about the company to its stakeholders and to the investment community at large. The decision not to invest may give any one or more of the following impressions:

- The business does not appear to want to grow.

- It wishes to preserve funds for future opportunities.

- It is risk averse.

- It sees no opportunities for development of current markets.

- It is quite happy to trade upon present activity but not to look to the future.

- It sees no benefits to employee morale from investment in capital assets.

---

### An example of the costs of *not* undertaking investment

James plc invested £2.5m in a plant to produce printed circuit boards, using new technology, although they had insufficient orders to justify the plant initially. The discounted, present value of the anticipated future cash flows amounted to only £2.0m, so the net present value of the project was negative. The financial argument was that the capital investment of £2.5m was too much to justify the commencement of the project. The commercially aware argument was that there are some investments that you have to make simply to stay in business in the future – regardless of the cost. The financial appraisal ignored the cost of the consequences of *not* investing in the new technology. For example:

- James will lose orders if they do not "keep up with the times" by acquiring and having knowledge of new technologies.
- James' staff will not have experience of the new technologies and their skills will eventually become out of date.
- James' costs will be higher than competitors if the new technology is more efficient.

---

It is difficult to quantify the cost of *not* making a particular strategic investment. The effect of such a decision not to invest may be quite dramatic – on the future business of the enterprise and upon its employees and customers.

## KEEPING ONE'S OPTIONS OPEN

One of the newer academic ideas in strategic investment appraisal is to look at the investment decision as an **option**. Senior managers may see that, by taking up a particular investment opportunity, they are keeping their options open with regard to opportunities that may be available in the future. Such an investment may currently have an expected NPV which is negative. That is, the initial cost of sustaining a presence in that market is higher than the present value of the cash flows that can reasonably be expected in the market in the foreseeable future. But there may be a time when the market for the product or service takes off – and high rewards can be expected – although it would be very difficult to *quantify* the value of such income now. The maintenance of a presence in the market, albeit with a negative net present value, is effectively keeping management's options open. Essentially the negative NPV is equal to the cost of having such flexibility.

Such an investment – with a negative NPV – has been likened to the purchase of a forward option for the purchase or sale of a share on the stock exchange or of foreign currency. In each case, the option is purchased so that managers may have the flexibility of undertaking some future transaction – if it is worthwhile to do so – or alternatively walking away from the situation. This is often the result of carrying out some scenario planning. If either of two situations could occur (as we saw in Chapter 2 p 41), one favourable, one adverse, it is a reasonable strategy to prepare for the best but anticipate the worst.

An option is purchased giving the holder the right to buy or sell at a particular price in the future. If the future price is right the option will be taken up. Whether the price is right or not depends upon whether or not you are buying or selling:

- **an option to buy.** A purchase option will give the holder the right to buy at a particular price at a future date. If the market price at that future date is higher, the holder of the option will take up the option and buy at the option price. If the future market price is lower than the option price, the holder of the option will obviously not take up the option, but will buy in the market at the lower market price.

- **an option to sell.** A sales option provides the right to sell at a particular price at a future date. If the future market price is lower than the option price, the holder of the option will sell at the option price. If the future market price is higher than the option price, the holder will ignore the option held and sell in the market at the higher price.

There is a cost, of course, of having the option to buy or sell (or not) at a given price in the future – the option premium. Obviously, the party on the other side of the option – the "writer" of the option – will only offer the option opportunity for a fee. The fee is called an option premium and is paid at the outset when the option is agreed between the writer and the subsequent holder of the option. The premium amount will depend upon expectations of future prices in a particular market and the amount of variability of prices in that market. The more fluctuations there are in the market prices of an asset or commodity generally, the higher the option premium, because there is a higher chance that the option will be called upon, from the writers' point of view.

The classic example of the use of this option theory in investment decisions is the purchase of part of a North Sea oil field (see panel below). In general, it is quite possible to argue that a project with a negative NPV should be undertaken because it offers the option of undertaking a further investment opportunity in the future. The cost of this option – the option premium – is the amount of negative NPV. The future opportunity may be the possibility to become involved in a future market for a product or service which *may* develop in the future. If the current (negative NPV) investment is not undertaken now, it will not be possible to enjoy the growth which may come later. On the other hand, if the possible developments are not forthcoming, the initial investment can be wound down – albeit at a cost, because of the original negative NPV. The organization will have had the opportunity to have been in a position to have gained if the future development had been a success. Examples are:

- Marketing managers may be reluctant to cease investment in a particular market. Although investment in that market currently would give negative NPVs, marketing managers want to maintain their position in the market.

## Option theory and oil fields

When the British and Norwegian governments were developing the North Sea oil fields, they sold the rights to prospect for oil by auction, block by block in the North Sea. Oil exploration companies who purchased rights were able to search for oil underneath the sea in their designated area. They did not know at the time of purchase of their block(s) of area of North Sea, whether or not they would find oil. The amount they paid for such exploration rights depended upon their assessment of the likelihood of finding oil – and more importantly perhaps how much.

What the oil companies were doing, in fact, was purchasing an option for oil *extraction*. The option premium amounted to the price they paid for the rights to explore in their particular block in the North Sea and the cost of exploration. The option was:

- to undertake extraction – if suitable quantities of oil were found;
- to cease further exploration if inadequate supplies of oil were discovered;
- to delay development of the oil field because the price of oil in international markets is too low for oil extraction to be profitable (as has happened recently).

If the option – the purchase of rights to explore – had not been purchased, no oil extraction could have been undertaken, by definition. By purchasing the right to explore, the oil company had the option to develop the field further or to wind down development in the area.

- Marketing managers consider that they should be seen to be part of a particular new market in spite of the fact that it is not yet profitable to be in it.
- Research and development managers may well continue in areas of product or service innovation or improvement which currently do not appear to have an obvious return. But continued research keeps the possibility of future success open; ceasing it closes down on that option.
- A trial production plant may be built in order to have the option to go into full, economic production later. The NPV of the test

plant because of its size – too small to be economically viable – will probably be negative.

# THE WIDER ISSUES

Good, complete project appraisal will bring into account all the relevant factors, including market trends, competitor behaviors, the effect upon employees' morale, and the effect of a major investment on the business as a whole. The cost of not undertaking the investment should also be taken into account. So it may be a question of defining the boundaries of the project. If managers feel that a project which appears to have a negative NPV is nonetheless worthwhile pursuing, it is probably necessary to retrace the financial analysis to see what other costs and benefits should be included in the base case numbers.

> **Good complete project appraisal will bring into account all the relevant factors, including market trends, competitor behaviors, the effect upon employees' morale, and the effect of a major investment on the business as a whole.**

This does not mean that managers should simply use their own opinions to make investment decisions – rather than use the financial data that they have available. They should not make investments based entirely on their "gut feel." Managers use their experience, their expertise, and their knowledge about the business *in addition to* the financial data at their disposal. All investment decisions are taken without certain knowledge of what is to happen in the future – what will be the exact effect of undertaking or not undertaking the investment. Whoever makes the decision, to some extent, is taking a leap in the dark, but that leap should be as well informed as possible.

> **Whoever makes the decision, to some extent, is taking a leap in the dark, but that leap should be as well informed as possible.**

It is also true that senior management may see something else in the opportunity that investment appraisal offers which cannot easily be expressed in the figures. There are a whole range of reasons that we proposed in Chapter 4 why investment decisions may have to be taken. These reasons we suggested were not solely for the purposes of immediate improvement in the profitability of a particular company.

Good project evaluation considers *all* the relevant factors, including all those hard-to-quantify costs and benefits. The classic quotation in strategic investment is: "Does the product or service provide enough value to a sufficient number of customers to support prices and volumes that exceed the cost of supplying it including an adequate return?" What needs to be added to that statement is that the adequate return should take into account the wider opportunity costs and benefits from the introduction of the product or service.

**Good project evaluation considers *all* the relevant factors, including all those hard-to-quantify costs and benefits.**

> A major pharmaceutical company decided to construct a large research laboratory in South Wales to seek to find improvements in the treatment of patients with heart conditions. The investment was considered to be an important signal to the market and the company's own employees of its continuing commitment to stay in this line of business.
>
> Staff morale throughout the company improved because staff regarded the company's long-term commitment to such pure research as having an effect upon their well-being and continuing employment in the longer term. Management found it difficult to express these benefits in "concrete" financial terms, but they "felt" that the benefits were there.

Managers taking a particular investment decision may well perceive that there are wider benefits of the investment (and in some cases wider cost implications). What managers need to do is carefully to define the boundaries of the project – but as widely as possible. In this way, the factors which are difficult to quantify, but are nonetheless important to the decision, will at least be considered by managers using their experience and judgment. These wider issues may be viewed from four different perspectives, as shown in Figure 8.1.

**Figure 8.1 Taking account of the wider issues**

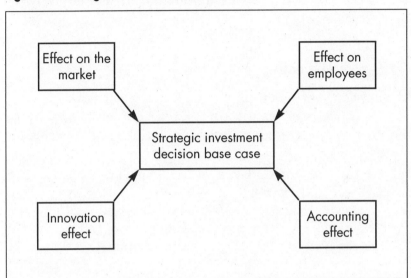

The four perspectives shown in Figure 8.1 may be described as follows:

## 1 Effect on the market

Projects which taken in their own right in isolation may indicate a poor return. If the wider implications of having that product or service available in a particular market are taken into account, it may well be that from the enterprise's point of view it is worthwhile that the project proceeds. Examples are:

- an "entry level" product in a market which is not greatly profitable but which sets up distribution and sales channels for more profitable products later. This may especially be the case when developing markets abroad.
- the maintenance of old-style products in a developed market in order to protect market share for the time being until new

products are introduced. Capital expenditure may be needed to replace plant and equipment in the established market which may show a poor return unless the longer-term, subsidiary implications are taken into account.

Hamel and Prahalad argue that a firm must "create" new ways of doing business.

## 2 Effect on the employees

The development of new production facilities may be an opportunity for staff to learn new skills or to learn about new technologies – which, in turn, may lead to greater profitability later. Any particular investment might be regarded not as an end in itself, but as a means of creating capabilities for the future of the business. In this way managers can be seen to be placing less emphasis on a particular investment decision, but rather on creating a strategic environment where employees are encouraged to develop their capabilities and are empowered to develop innovative ideas. The value of the development of this human capital cannot readily be quantified and it may therefore fall to managers to take these aspects into account in their management judgment.

## 3 Innovation effect

The wider implications of creating an innovative environment are of major importance today. With seemingly constant change the management of such change is arguably the greatest challenge in business now. Innovation affects not only the products that are sold and how they are made, but also the way that they are sold and the services offered around them. In fact, innovation in the provision of services has been the outstanding feature of business in the last ten years. Contracting out, compulsory competitive tendering, automated services (such as automated teller machines) and direct selling have become recognized processes in service provision.

In as far as innovation may be regarded these days as the introduction of new technology, the panel describes how such change may be regarded in a market.

---

### ◆ DISRUPTIVE VERSUS SUSTAINING TECHNOLOGIES ◆

The introduction of new technology into a market has been described as being either a "disruptive" technology or a "sustaining" technology. Disruptive technologies are so called because when they are introduced into a market they change the way that customers carry out their business. Sustaining technologies, on the other hand, only relate to improvements of products which are already used by customers and thus tend not to change the nature of their business.

Risk is reduced by providing customers with improvements to conventional products – those that they already know. But if it is perceived that there is a market for an entirely new product, or that there will be one at some time, it may be necessary to invest in disruptive innovations rather than simply going along with the current flow.

---

What managers have to consider in assessing investment opportunities involving innovative ideas are the effects on their business as a whole – and particularly in the longer term. IBM ignored the personal computer (PC) initially because they felt that the market for PCs (a major innovation in the computer market as it turned out) would be too small for them to be involved. They needed to assess correctly the wider effects on the computer market of the innovation of the PC. Of course, it is easy in retrospect to see the effect of the changes that took place – it was not so easy at the time!

Appreciating the effects of innovative ideas, while being absolutely vital for successful business management, may be regarded as just good guesswork! Such assessment should be thought of as sound management judgment.

To some extent this echoes "Gestalt" theory, which is concerned with being able to see the whole picture from separate parts and making linkage – not obvious if the spotlight is on a single issue. "Holism" could well describe this skill.

## 4 Accounting effect

Where a new product or service uses materials or components made in other production departments in a group of companies, it may be worthwhile to produce the new product even though alone it appears not to be highly profitable. The effect of the production of extra components in those other departments of the company will have two main effects:

1 Overheads will be spread over a greater number of units of production
2 Greater efficiency of production plant may be achieved

Overheads for each of the production departments will be spread over a greater production, thus improving the profitability of the company overall. Break-even analysis shows how profits are increased as there are more units produced over which to spread the overheads. The example in the Appendix to this chapter illustrates this point. The extra units of a new component or product may just make the plant viable in terms of its profitability by spreading that plant's overheads over more units. Therefore, if the new product, which may have looked unprofitable on its own, is introduced, the benefits are wider than might otherwise have been foreseen and when brought into account make it worthwhile to introduce the new item into production.

There may well be technical advantages of extra production – longer production runs, keeping the plant running continuously and so on. Longer production runs mean that there is less down time setting up machinery for the manufacture of different products or components. Often plant that runs more or less continuously works better than plant which is often stopping and starting.

The larger organization will also be better able to manage the full weight of general overheads or "head office" costs – such as corporate management, corporate marketing, and legal and financial support. The more these often hefty costs can be spread throughout the organization, the lighter the individual load will be.

# CONCLUSION

"Great manufacturing strategies are built on unique skills and capabilities, not on investments in buildings, equipment or specific individuals."[1] This chapter has argued that there may be very many other issues that management needs to take into account when looking at a specific investment decision. There may be many reasons why managers wish to encourage a particular investment decision, whether or not in its own right it appears to be financially viable. It may be a question of keeping one's options open or of spreading some of the overheads of the company but these are issues that managers should take into account as well as taking on board the financial information available.

It is likely that particular strategic investments will have effects on the business as a whole and will effectively assist managers in growing the value of the business. In recent years, attempts have been made to measure the value of a business taking a long-term perspective and it is to those techniques – and how they might be used in the appraisal of strategic investments – that we turn in Chapter 9.

# APPENDIX: BREAK-EVEN ANALYSIS

Tie-Shop plc purchase ties at an average cost of £10 and sell them for £15. Their overheads – selling, marketing and administrative costs – may be regarded as "fixed" and amount to £18m per year. Fixed costs in accounting terminology are costs which do not vary (certainly in the short run) with the amount of business done. Variable costs, on the other hand, vary directly with the level of business activity. In the case of Tie-Shop, every time a tie is sold, there is a variable cost of £10, but the fixed costs of £18m are unaltered.

Eventually, of course, with expansion, the fixed costs will need to be increased. Let us assume that the £18m overheads allow for 400 retail outlets, each of which can be expected to sell no more than 12,000 ties per year. If the company wishes to increase its sales, more retail outlets would have to be opened and the fixed costs would increase accordingly. Staff costs and premises costs would increase as a lump sum.

The "contribution" (the difference between selling price and variable cost) for each tie on average is £5 (selling price £15 – cost price

---

[1] Hayes and Pisano, Harvard Business Review, January/February 1994.

£10). If the present fixed costs are £18m, it is clear that 3.6m ties (£18m/£5) have to be sold in order for Tie-Shop to break even:

|  |  | £m |
|---|---|---|
| Sales | 3.6m × £15 | 54.0 |
| Cost of sales | 3.6m × £10 | 36.0 |
| Contribution |  | 18.0 |
| Fixed overhead costs |  | 18.0 |
| Net profit |  | nil |

If the volume of business is (hopefully) greater than 3.6m ties per year, we can show that as the volume increases, the profit *per unit* of product (ties, in this case), increases dramatically. Consider the following:

| *Sales (ties)* | 4.0m | 4.4m | 4.8m* |
|---|---|---|---|
|  | £m | £m | £m |
| Sales | 60.0 | 66.0 | 72.0 |
| Cost of sales | 40.0 | 44.0 | 48.0 |
| Contribution | 20.0 | 22.0 | 24.0 |
| Fixed costs | 18.0 | 18.0 | 18.0 |
| Net profit | 2.0 | 4.0 | 6.0 |
| Net profit per unit (average) | 50p | 91p | 1.25p |

* Maximum sales are 4.8m ties (400 shops × 12,000 ties each)

Thus not only does the total profit increase with increased volume, but the profit *per tie* increases dramatically. This is because the £18m overheads are spread progressively over more and more units.

Compare the overheads *per unit* at the break-even point and at the present maximum trading level:

At break-even the cost per unit of overheads is £5: At full capacity the cost per unit of overheads is £3.75 – quite a difference.

|  | Break-even level | Full capacity level |
|---|---|---|
| Sales (units) | 3.6m | 4.8m |
| *Per unit figures* | | |
|  | £ | £ |
| Sales | 15.0 | 15.0 |
| Cost of sales | 10.0 | 10.0 |
| Contribution | 5.0 | 5.0 |
| Fixed costs | 5.0 (18/3.6) | 3.75 (18/4.8) |
| Net profit | nil | 1.25 |

The profit of £6m at full capacity looked at one way is the result of the extra *contribution* from the units sold after the break-even point:

4.8m units (full capacity) – 3.6m (break-even capacity) × £5 = £6m

Alternatively, the profit can be seen to arise from spreading the overheads over more units – and thus reducing the cost per unit, including fixed costs – as follows:

|  | £ |
|---|---|
| Fixed costs per unit at break-even | 5.00 |
| Fixed costs per unit at full capacity | 3.75 |
| Cost saving from spreading overheads | 1.25 |
| Sales volume at full capacity | 4.8m |
| Profit at full capacity (£1.25 × 4.8m) | 6.0m |

"At the end of the day what matters with an investment is whether it fits in with what is considered to be the strategic development of the firm."

# Chapter 9

◆

# DOES THE INVESTMENT FIT IN WITH OUR STRATEGIC PLANS?

At the end of the day what matters with an investment is whether it fits in with what is considered to be the strategic development of the firm. There is absolutely no point in making a capital investment in plant and machinery unless it is expected that the particular equipment will be needed in the business over the longer term. This is because of the nature of capital investment. It is made now for the future and cannot easily be reversed. It is inflexible. The cost cannot be avoided by making it redundant because most of the cost has been spent at the commencement of the project. The cost of plant purchased to make components or products or to mine mineral resources cannot be undone if, subsequently, it is decided that those products or raw materials are no longer required. If, at some later stage, it is considered that the production of particular products or materials no longer fit the long-term strategy of the business, then the capital investment in the related production facilities will have been a mistake. It is therefore vital that the capital investment decision is set in the context of the long-term strategic plans of the investing organization.

> It is therefore vital that the capital investment decision is set in context of the long-term strategic plans of the investing organization.

Fortunately, the strategic decision comes before the strategic investment. Ideally, the need is to create distinctive situations

169

where the skills and capabilities of the organization might be made unique and therefore will enable a company to make higher than average profits. Shareholder value can only be created from imperfections and inequalities in the market – achieved by competitive advantage strategies. Firms should be seeking investments that make a company unique in this sense.

So the aim will be to seek strategies which will set the company apart from others in the industry. In this way, economic value will be added to the enterprise. Investments which enter into this framework – to give the firm distinctive characteristics – can be said to have "strategic fit" with the long-term plans of the business. Such investments will be less likely to be wasted because they will be in sympathy with the aims which the whole organization is pursuing. At the very least, this will be the case until the whole strategy of the company changes.

# STRATEGIC FIT

The nature of the whole organization may provide a clue as to whether or not a particular capital investment will fit the longer-term strategy. Many companies have their own peculiar style which affects their business development. Companies develop quite different overall impressions as can be seen from looking at very many different types of companies that exist in the world. Consider two distinguishing characteristics of different sorts of company: the investment in different types of new technology and the degree of diversification undertaken.

- In terms of investment in new technology, companies range from those who decide upon low-tech business to those who aggressively seek opportunities in hi-tech activities. Arguably, low-tech business is less risky, whereas hi-tech business involves more risk. Each type of activity may therefore attract different types of corporate management.

- Another distinction in company styles relates to the degree of specialization practiced. Enterprises range from highly diversified companies to companies which specialize in one particular industry.

Figure 9.1 provides examples of specific industry sectors differentiated by the type of technological investment and by the degree of

**Figure 9.1**

| Corporate strategic styles | | |
|---|---|---|
| | *Specialized* | *Diversified* |
| Hi-tech | Computer systems manufacturers, pharmaceutical (drugs) manufacturers | Electronic components manufacturers, office equipment suppliers |
| Low-tech | Food retailers, hotel groups, drinks manufacturers (some), car manufacturers | Engineering companies, construction companies, diversified industrials (i.e., most conglomerates) |

diversification. The examples provided are somewhat generalized. There are, of course, specialized, hi-tech motorcar manufacturers – for example, Lotus and Ferrari! There are also engineering companies which employ advanced technology.

So when a particular investment proposal is under consideration, it is sensible to consider whether the specific *type* of investment has, on the face of it, "strategic fit" with the style of company concerned (see panel). It is unlikely that an investment in pure medical research (specialized, hi-tech) would fit in well in a company producing a range of building material products (relatively low-tech and fairly well diversified).

An example of a situation where an investment did not appear to have a natural strategic fit was that of Tomkins plc's purchase of RHM. Tomkins is a fast-growing diversified industrial company, concerned with the production of a very wide range of industrial products including valves and suchlike for fluid controls, material handling equipment, lawn mowers and "a range of niche, low-risk technology products." Turnover had increased over the ten years to April 1993 from £25.9m to £2,059.5m. The purchase of a major food processing and packaging group (RHM) did not appear to match the type of investment normally pursued by Tomkins. The move from making general engineering products to food processing was considered to be a change in their strategic direction. They were moving into a business that they did not have experience in. Such an investment was regarded by some commentators to have little "strategic fit" with their conventional business activity.

But was it such a step? The food processing and packaging business is essentially low-tech, so perhaps the purchase of RHM by Tomkins was not really very extraordinary for the group. In the event, the acquisition has been successful – certainly in terms of the financial results – and it could be argued that any acquisition would fit into the structure of a conglomerate organization. Diversified industrial groups essentially create a management control environment in which, theoretically, any business can be incorporated.

# EVALUATION OF THE WHOLE STRATEGY

If we assume that a particular investment proposal seems to possess an apparent strategic fit with business as a whole, clearly what is needed is a means of being able to judge whether, in financial terms, the enterprise as a whole will benefit from it. We make the assumption here that the financial appraisal of the project on a *stand alone basis* has already been carried out. The question is: How can all the other aspects of the project that were discussed in Chapter 8 be included in the financial analysis? That is, can they be brought into the *evaluation* of the project? It is possible that the project and its effect on the whole business can be shown to be worthwhile, if a wide enough perspective is taken. Furthermore, it may be that the length of time over which the project (and its effect) is assessed is very material to the decision.

It may be the case that a project which looks marginal from a financial point of view, but yet appears to have strategic fit, could be shown to be of benefit to the company, if all factors are taken into account. On the other hand, can we be sure that a project which meets financial criteria set by the company's management will actually add value to that company, if the overall impact of the introduction of the project is considered? The valuation model which will allow us to evaluate the company wide effects of strategic investment is based on shareholder value analysis. Shareholder value analysis (SVA) encourages managers to consider the longer-term effects of their actions, as well as the short-term costs and benefits. As it is concerned with the process of the valuation of the business as a whole, it also raises questions about the effect of a project upon the financial results of the whole enterprise.

173

# SHAREHOLDER VALUE ANALYSIS

Shareholder value analysis (SVA) was developed to measure the value of a company's shares at a particular point in time. Its development into a tool which measures strategic plans is relatively new and there are few published examples of how companies have used the technique in this way in practice. As a means of evaluating particular investments from a strategic point of view, however, SVA is very useful. Instead of assessing whether or not a particular investment should be adopted – taking that investment in isolation – SVA is a process which enables the investment to be set into the strategic context of the firm as a whole.

**SVA is a process which enables the investment to be set into the strategic context of the firm as a whole.**

SVA uses the same discounting process outlined earlier. Corporate value is established by discounting the future cash flows that are expected to be generated by the business as a whole. The cash flow that is discounted is essentially the annual cash flow from trading less taxation, allowing for capital expenditure and for movements in working capital. Table 9.1 sets out the process for

**Table 9.1**

| The cash flow computation in shareholder value analysis | |
|---|---|
| **Basis of the cash flow each year** | **Reasons for inclusion in the computation** |
| Net profit for year before interest and taxation | Source of cash flow – that is, from trading |
| *multiplied by* | |
| 1-corporate tax rate | to establish *after-tax* cash flows |
| *plus* | |
| depreciation and other "allocations" | non-cash charges to profit are added back to establish the *cash flow* generated from trading |
| *minus* | |
| capital expenditures and the cash required for any increase in working capital taken year by year. | to allow for the capital expenditure and extra working capital required to maintain trading activity and for growth of the business. |

calculating the annual cash flows needed for an SVA computation. The table summarises why each of the items appear in the calculation.

Once the cash flows have been calculated for each year, they are discounted in just the same way as cash flows are to evaluate individual projects. But in SVA, the result is different from that of project appraisal. From Table 9.1, it can be seen that capital expenditure for the entire business is taken into account *over the years* – as and when it is needed to replace worn out assets and for the growth of the business. In individual project appraisal, the capital expenditure required for the project is usually deducted in total from the total present value of the project cash flows – to see whether there is a positive or negative net present value. The result in SVA is effectively the same – a net present value of the firm – a business value – is established from this process.

The major difference in the computation of corporate value in this way, compared to that used in investment appraisal is that, in the case of the business as a whole, cash flow may be expected to be forthcoming for many years to come. For an individual project it is realistic to assume that cash flows cease after the end of the economic life of the project. For calculation purposes, what is usually assumed in SVA is that cash flows for the enterprise are estimated over what is considered to be a reasonable planning period for the company – probably five to ten years. After that a continuing value of the business is assumed. The present value of this continuing value is added to the present value of the cash flows generated during the planning period to establish the full business value.

The whole process of SVA calculations is much the same as it is for individual investment appraisal. The two methods are compared in Table 9.2.

As Table 9.2 shows, the process of valuing the whole company is very similar to that of evaluating an investment within the company. Estimates have to be made about the expected cash flows, about the length of the economic life of the investment and of the residual value at the end of its economic life. However, developing the cash flow scenario for a corporate valuation, two factors influence the forecasts greatly:

**Table 9.2**

| The cash flow computation in shareholder value analysis | | |
| --- | --- | --- |
| Steps in the analysis | Corporate valuation using SVA | Investment appraisal using DCF |
| 1 Establish the cash flows | Net profit before interest and taxation with depreciation added back, estimated over the planning period | Estimated revenues and costs (excluding depreciation over the life of the project |
| | *minus* | *minus* |
| 2 Taxation | Corporate taxation on the corporate profits | Estimated tax payable on project income |
| | *minus* | *minus* |
| 3 Capital expenditure | Capital expenditure required to maintain the level of business and for the growth of the company | Capital expenditure required (usually at the outset) for the project |
| | *minus* | *minus* |
| 4 Working capital expenditure | Expenditure on working capital as the level of business increases | Expenditure on working capital over the life of the project (which may all be recovered at the end of the project) |
| | *plus* | *plus* |
| 5 Continuing value | Value of the business at the end of the planning period | Sale value of any assets at the end of the life of the project |
| 6 Discounting | Sum total for both is discounted at the cost of capital | |
| | *to equal* | *to equal* |
| 7 Result | Value of the business | Net present value |

1 For how long ahead can we be reasonably expected to estimate detailed cash flows associated with the company?

2 How is the value of the business at the end of this planning period to be established or estimated?

Consider the case study of the Allied Shoe Corporation by way of an example. It shows how SVA can be used to evaluate the plans for a business as a whole, where one (fairly large) investment is being decided upon.

# CASE STUDY

The Allied Shoe Corporation is a manufacturer of footwear which was started by Tom Cooper's father in 1950. The company has always been a specialist shoe manufacturers concentrating on fairly low production quantities, but with flexible facilities which can react quickly to new fashion designs and public demand. During the 1980s the company was drawn in particular into the sports and leisure footwear market. They became very well known in the sporting world for original lightweight football boots, golfing shoes, loafers, and the like.

The forecast level of sales for the company for the current year amounts to £75.6m, with an anticipated final profit figure by the end of the year of £3.78m. A summarized trading account forecast to be the result of the current year's activities is shown in Table 9.3.

**Table 9.3**

| Forecast trading account of Allied Shoe Corporation | | |
|---|---|---|
| | £000s | % Sales |
| Sales turnover | 75,600 | 100.0 |
| Cost of sales | 53,827 | 71.2 |
| Gross profit | 21,773 | 28.8 |
| Operating expenses | 17,993 | 23.8 |
| Operating profit | 3,780 | 5.0 |

The value of the company's equity, as at the end of the current year, based on these figures, could be estimated using SVA. From the recent sales history of Allied Shoe and taking a view about future growth in sales, the assumption is made that turnover will grow by about 5 percent for the next five years. It is assumed that no further growth in the business takes place after five years. (This case study assumes a planning period of only five years, simply to restrict the calculations involved. We do realize that this is a particularly short period over which to assess the value of a business.) If further assumptions are made about the cost of sales, operating expenses and the amounts of capital expenditure required in the business and so on, the corporate value of Allied Shoe at the end of the current year can be estimated.

Table 9.4 sets out how this calculation could be made and shows that an estimated corporate value of Allied Shoe would be £32.3m. The following assumptions and explanations are needed for some of the calculations in Table 9.4:

- The forecast results of the current year are shown in the first column of figures.
- Sales revenues are expected to increase at 5 percent per year for the five-year planning period, but not thereafter.
- Estimates are made (for the five-year planning period) of the percentage cost of sales and operating expenses.
- Depreciation is forecast to be £1,826,000 in Year 1 and increases by 5 percent per year in line with sales – a simplifying assumption but nonetheless adequate for our purposes here.
- Capital expenditure required for replacing the assets that are depreciating and for the growth in sales is assumed to be £2,620,000 in Year 1 and it increases by 5 percent per year also in line with sales.
- Extra working capital will also be needed as the business grows. There will be an estimated increase in inventory and debtors (receivables) amounting to 15 percent of the *extra* sales each year.
- The corporate cash flow for each year is calculated as the sum of income and expenditure under the above assumptions plus the value of the cash flows expected after the end of the five-year

**Table 9.4**

## Current situation

| £000s | Current year £ | Budgeted % of sales | Year 1 £ | Year 2 £ | Year 3 £ | Year 4 £ | Year 5 £ | Year 5 onwards £ |
|---|---|---|---|---|---|---|---|---|
| Sales | 75,600 | | 79,380 | 83,349 | 87,516 | 91,892 | 96,487 | |
| Cost of sales | 53,827 | 71.0 | 56,360 | 59,178 | 62,137 | 65,244 | 68,506 | |
| Gross profit | 21,773 | | 23,020 | 24,171 | 25,380 | 26,649 | 27,981 | |
| Operating expenses | 17,993 | 23.5 | 18,654 | 19,587 | 20,566 | 21,595 | 22,674 | |
| Operating profit | 3,780 | 5.5 | 4,366 | 4,584 | 4,813 | 5,054 | 5,307 | |
| Taxation (33% of profit) | | | 1,441 | 1,513 | 1,588 | 1,668 | 1,751 | |
| Net profit after taxation | | | 2,925 | 3,071 | 3,225 | 3,386 | 3,556 | 3,556 |
| Depreciation | | | 1,826 | 1,917 | 2,013 | 2,114 | 2,219 | in perpetuity |
| Operating cash flow | | | 4,751 | 4,988 | 5,238 | 5,500 | 5,775 | |
| Capital expenditure | | | (2,620) | (2,751) | (2,888) | (3,032) | (3,184) | |
| Working capital | | | (567) | (595) | (625) | (656) | (689) | |
| Corporate cash flow | | | 1,564 | 1,642 | 1,725 | 1,812 | 1,902 | 39,511 |
| Discounted at 9% | | | 1,435 | 1,383 | 1,332 | 1,283 | 1,236 | 25,680 |

Total present value of cash flows = corporate value = 32,349 (£32.3m)

planning period. The continuing value of the business in this case, is taken to be the value of £3,556,000 in perpetuity. What this means is that the assumption being made is that after Year 5 the operating cash flow of £3,556,000 will continue forever without any growth. Any "depreciation cash" will be used to replace assets when they become too old, so that the business will self-perpetuate as far as one can see into the future.

The value of a sum receivable in perpetuity is obtained by dividing through by the rate of interest required. In the case of Allied Shoe the cost of capital and the required rate of return is assumed to be 9 percent, so the value of £3,556,000, as from the beginning of Year 5 is:

$$\frac{3,556,000}{0.09} = £39,511,000$$

• the corporate cash flow is then discounted at 9 percent and all the discounted cash flows are summed to obtain the corporate value of £32,349,000 as shown in Table 9.4.

## The investment opportunity

The company has the opportunity to purchase a new factory next year to produce a new-style football boot which they have designed. The sales of the new boot could only be expected to last for five years – before a new design was introduced – which is again an oversimplification. The new factory building will cost £1.35m and equipment and plant needed to produce the football boot will cost £420,000. The plant will be worthless (fully depreciated) at the end of five years but for the purposes of the evaluation of the football boot investment it is assumed that the factory building will be "sold" for £1.35m in five years' time.

Table 9.5 shows discounted cash flow analysis for the football boot investment – indicating that the net present value of the investment is in fact negative! The management team of Allied Shoe, nonetheless, would like to go ahead with the investment. They feel that the new boot will widen their product range and that it will provide a secure and regular cash flow over five years. They also have their eyes on the new factory. They see that as a means of increasing their

**Table 9.5**

| The football boot investment | | | | | |
|---|---|---|---|---|---|
| £000s | Year 1 | Year 2 | Year 3 | Year 4 | Year 5 |
| | £ | £ | £ | £ | £ |
| Sales | 1,350 | 1,450 | 1,025 | 590 | 380 |
| Manufacturing costs | 891 | 957 | 676 | 389 | 251 |
| Gross profit | 459 | 493 | 349 | 201 | 129 |
| Directly attributable expenses | 270 | 330 | 300 | 190 | 180 |
| Operating profit of project | 189 | 163 | 49 | 11 | (51) |
| Taxation (as calculated re project) | | 28 | 28 | (3) | (11)* |
| Net profit after taxation paid | 189 | 135 | 21 | 14 | (40) |
| Depreciation | 84 | 84 | 84 | 84 | 84 |
| Cash flow from project after tax | 273 | 219 | 105 | 98 | 44 |
| Capital expenditure | (1,770) | | | | 1,350 † |
| Working capital | (203) | (15) | 64 | 65 | 89 |
| Project cash flow, allowing for capital expenditure | (1,700) | 204 | 168 | 163 | 1,483 |
| Discounted at 9% | (1,559) | 172 | 130 | 116 | 964 |

Total present value of
  cash flows
  = net present value = (177)

* Tax on Year 5 profits paid later has been ignored; as have continuing capital allowances.
† Value of property at the end of Year 5.

production capacity – for other new products – and thus as an opportunity to grow the business more quickly than presently expected.

Table 9.6 shows the effect of combining the project with its negative NPV with the value of the business as a whole. On the face of it, the corporate value of Allied Shoe falls by the negative NPV of the project, so that the corporate value of the company becomes £32.2m – compared with £32.3m originally.

Before the decision is taken to abort the proposed investment to manufacture the football boot, the board wish to consider the *wider* issues suggested by the proposal. The board have two *strategies* in mind which they wish to evaluate:

1 the further expansion possible if the new factory is acquired.

2 the undertaking of a major reorganization of the company's current production facilities.

## Strategy 1: Further expansion

The whole floor area of the new factory will not be taken up by the equipment needed for the production of the new football boot. The board estimate that they will be able to use the spare floor area to provide manufacturing facilities for additional production of their main products and for a number of new (yet unspecified) products. This will allow them to expand sales at a rate of 9 percent over the next five years rather than the 5 percent originally envisaged. This is as well as providing capacity for the football boot investment.

Table 9.7 shows that the corporate value viewed from the end of the current year taking into account these expansion plans amounts to £36.2m. So Allied Shoe would add £4.0m to its value – more than 12 percent of its value before these alternative plans were considered! This is the case in spite of undertaking an investment which, taken in its own right and isolated from the wider perspective, has a negative net present value.

## Strategy 2: Reorganization of current production facilities

Rather than investing in the new factory and the equipment to make the new football boot, the board has an alternative strategy

**Table 9.6**

## Combined investment

| £000s | Current year £ | Year 1 £ | Year 2 £ | Year 3 £ | Year 4 £ | Year 5 £ | Year 5 onwards £ |
|---|---|---|---|---|---|---|---|
| Sales | 75,600 | 80,730 | 84,799 | 88,541 | 92,482 | 96,867 | |
| Cost of sales | 53,827 | 57,251 | 60,135 | 62,813 | 65,633 | 68,757 | |
| Gross profit | 21,773 | 23,479 | 24,664 | 25,728 | 26,850 | 28,110 | |
| Operating expenses | 17,993 | 18,924 | 19,917 | 20,866 | 21,785 | 22,854 | |
| Operating profit | 3,780 | 4,555 | 4,747 | 4,862 | 5,065 | 5,256 | |
| Taxation | | 1,441 | 1,541 | 1,616 | 1,664 | 1,740 | |
| Net profit after taxation | | 3,114 | 3,206 | 3,246 | 3,400 | 3,516 | 3,556 in perpetuity |
| Depreciation | | 1,910 | 2,001 | 2,097 | 2,198 | 2,303 | |
| Operating cash flow | | 5,024 | 5,207 | 5,343 | 5,598 | 5,819 | |
| Capital expenditure | | (4,390) | (2,751) | (2,888) | (3,032) | (1,834) | |
| Working capital | | (770) | (610) | (561) | (591) | (600) | |
| Corporate cash flow | | (135) | 1,846 | 1,893 | 1,975 | 3,385 | 39,511 |
| Discounted at 9% | | (124) | 1,554 | 1,462 | 1,399 | 2,200 | 25,680 |

Total present value of cash flows = corporate value = 32,171 (£32.2m)

**Table 9.7**

| £000s | Current year £ | Year 1 £ | Year 2 £ | Year 3 £ | Year 4 £ | Year 5 £ | Year 5 onwards £ |
|---|---|---|---|---|---|---|---|
| | | **Additional growth** | | | | | |
| Sales | 75,600 | 83,754 | 91,270 | 98,929 | 107,306 | 116,700 | |
| Cost of sales | 53,827 | 59,398 | 64,729 | 70,188 | 76,158 | 82,838 | |
| Gross profit | 21,773 | 24,356 | 26,541 | 28,741 | 31,148 | 33,862 | |
| Operating expenses | 17,993 | 19,635 | 21,768 | 23,608 | 25,458 | 27,695 | |
| Operating profit | 3,780 | 4,721 | 5,103 | 5,433 | 5,880 | 6,347 | |
| Taxation | | 1,495 | 1,658 | 1,805 | 1,933 | 2,100 | |
| Net profit after taxation | | 3,226 | 3,445 | 3,628 | 3,947 | 4,247 | 4,286 |
| Depreciation | | 1,979 | 2,150 | 2,336 | 2,538 | 2,759 | in perpetuity |
| Operating cash flow | | 5,205 | 5,595 | 5,964 | 6,485 | 7,006 | |
| Capital expenditure | | (4,489) | (2,964) | (3,231) | (3,522) | (2,489) | |
| Working capital | | (1,223) | (1,127) | (1,149) | (1,256) | (1,352) | |
| Corporate cash flow | | (507) | 1,504 | 1,584 | 1,707 | 3,165 | 47,627 |
| Discounted at 9% | | (466) | 1,265 | 1,224 | 1,209 | 2,057 | 30,954 |

Total present value of cash flows = corporate value = 36,243 (£36.2m)

which is more conservative. This plan would entail a reorganization of present production facilities and would mean that there would be no need to purchase the new premises and there would be no new football boot.

The aim of the reorganizations would be to reduce the cost of sales and operating expenses as a percentage of sales. For the purposes of budgeting over the planning period, the managers have estimated that the cost of sales figures for all its products could be reduced as follows:

|  | % Sales |
|---|---|
| Current year | 71.2 |
| Year 1 | 71.0 |
| Year 2 | 70.7 |
| Year 3 onwards | 70.5 |

The reorganization of the mostly fixed marketing and administrative costs will enable operating expenses to fall to 23.0 percent of sales.

If such a reorganization policy were pursued, and if it assumed that sales will not grow at all over the next five years, Table 9.8 shows that the corporate value of Allied Shoe, under this scenario, is expected to be £36.2m. This is the same as the value created if the expansion is undertaken!

Whether or not the board of Allied Shoe would take the decision to invest in the new premises to make the new football boot would be a question of their management judgment. The "further expansion" strategy looks economically less attractive than the "reorganization" strategy because a growth strategy has a higher degree of risk than a rationalization strategy. However the wider implications of reorganization – the effect on staff morale, for example – have to be considered.

What is clearer from this analysis is that management is better informed. The football project is not taken in isolation; the future of the whole business is considered. We can see the value of the business that is achieved in five years' time from each strategy. Perhaps this is what matters – the size of the future value of the business. If only business managers could persuade the financial markets that their business will grow substantially over the planning period,

**Table 9.8**

## Cost saving alternative

| £000s | Current year £ | Budgeted % of sales | Year 1 £ | Year 2 £ | Year 3 £ | Year 4 £ | Year 5 £ | Year 5 onwards £ |
|---|---|---|---|---|---|---|---|---|
| Sales | 75,600 | changing | 75,600 | 75,600 | 75,600 | 75,600 | 75,600 | |
| Cost of sales | 53,827 | | 53,676 | 53,449 | 53,298 | 53,298 | 53,298 | |
| Gross profit | 21,773 | | 21,924 | 22,151 | 22,302 | 22,302 | 22,302 | |
| Operating expenses | 17,993 | 23.0 | 17,388 | 17,388 | 17,388 | 17,388 | 17,388 | |
| Operating profit | 3,780 | | 4,536 | 4,763 | 4,914 | 4,914 | 4,914 | |
| Taxation (33% of profit) | | | 1,497 | 1,572 | 1,622 | 1,622 | 1,622 | |
| Net profit after taxation | | | 3,039 | 3,191 | 3,292 | 3,292 | 3,292 | 3,292 |
| Depreciation | | | 1,739 | 1,739 | 1,739 | 1,739 | 1,739 | in perpetuity |
| Operating cash flow | | | 4,778 | 4,930 | 5,031 | 5,031 | 5,031 | |
| Capital expenditure | | | (1,739) | (1,739) | (1,739) | (1,739) | (1,739) | |
| Working capital | | | 0 | 0 | 0 | 0 | 0 | |
| Corporate cash flow | | | 3,039 | 3,191 | 3,292 | 3,292 | 3,292 | 36,582 |
| Discounted at 9% | | | 2,788 | 2,686 | 2,542 | 2,332 | 2,140 | 23,776 |

Total present value of cash flows = corporate value = 36,264 (£36.2m)

perhaps they could persuade the market to overlook the results during the planning period!

For example, the combined results of Allied Shoe including the football boot investment (see Table 9.6) show a negative cash flow in Year 1, but the business value grows from £32.2m now to £39.5m at the end of Year 5 without taking the other growth potential into account. If the growth strategy is pursued, the value of the business in five years' time is £47.6m (see Table 9.7).

# CONCLUSION

The framework for analyzing strategic investment proposals suggested in this chapter shows how the wider issues *can* be incorporated into the financial appraisal. The shareholder value approach, which emphasizes building the value of the whole business, is a way to highlight the benefits that might ensue from the investment in a particular strategy. Instead of the investment being looked at in isolation, estimates of its effect on the cash flows of the whole business and thus its effect on shareholder value can be included.

Certainly many companies now express, often as part of their mission statement, a desire to maximize value for their shareholders. By using SVA methods to evaluate strategic performance, they can see how to *measure* or, at least, estimate the future value of the business for the shareholders.

♦

The greater the potential
reward, the greater the risk.

♦

Risk increases the further you go
away from your core business.

♦

# Chapter 10

◆

# STRATEGIC
# MANAGEMENT IN
# PRACTICE

In large companies these days, matters strategic are taken seriously, although the disappointing performance of many companies since the recession of the early 1990s suggests that not all handle the process as effectively as shareholders would like, nor as top management would desire. A similar view may be taken with regard to smaller companies, though the excuse which may be offered is that their resources – at senior level in particular – make the process that has been described in this book difficult to undertake, mainly because of the lack of time. Too much time is devoted to managing today's problems – or sorting out those from yesterday. This chapter offers some suggestions as to how strategic planning might be tackled, recognizing that all companies will have different situations and differing structures.

# WHOSE PROBLEM IS IT?

Initially the responsibility for the strategic framework must be with the board of directors, or the board of the subsidiary where profit and investment responsibilities are decentralized. The specific tasks are:

- establishing a vision
- stating the corporate mission
- setting objectives

## Establish a vision

The vision describes what kind of an organization is wanted in the future, in terms of its range of activities and its style. This needs to be articulated and discussed fully by the board. To a great extent the vision will be most clearly expressed by those board members who have been involved with the company for many years. Their vision may conflict with that of newer members, especially if the company has been through a takeover or buy-out. The vision has to make sense in the context of the world in which the company exists and should not be unrealistic. Moreover it should reflect the personal values of the senior management – the underlying personal beliefs which will determine how the company should carry out its tasks. Values are the criteria for deciding what is, or is not, acceptable practice.

> **Values are the criteria for deciding what is, or is not, acceptable practice.**

## State the corporate mission

The mission statement will describe in general terms how the vision is to be achieved – the direction which the company should take. Again there has to be agreement at board level and the statement must make sense to everyone in the organization. Too often mission statements are presented to the staff in a company as though they were "tablets of stone" sent from heaven. The board decides the mission, but after consultation.

## Set objectives

When setting objectives it is important to bear in mind, that they have to be realistic, but at the same time must be challenging. The idea of "stretch goals" suggests that companies need to be ambitious in their aims. All too often firms (and individuals) fail to achieve what they have set out to do. There seems to be no acceptable excuse for being corporately undemanding. To be useful, objectives must have several features:

> **There seems to be no acceptable excuse for being corporately undemanding.**

- The time horizon will be far enough into the future to enable strategic investment decisions to be implemented, yet should not be so far off that everything about the firm's environment will be unpredictable.

- Objectives must be defined precisely, without ambiguity.

- The specific items which are identified as objectives must be measurable and must have values assigned to them. The "hockey-stick" trap must be avoided. This is the (all too common) feature of having for several years a modest progression from today's position, followed by a quantum increase the year before the end of the planning horizon.

- If the achievement of the aims and objectives of the firm is dependent on the managerial skills of staff below board level, then their views have to be considered at the formulation stage. A cynical view often expressed is that boards set unrealistic aims, but that managers set easy targets. This does happen, but can only be overcome if there is a real debate, backed by facts not solely by opinions. At the end, directors have to set the objectives and ensure that they are properly communicated. They need to be ambitious, but realistic.

# WHERE ARE WE?

The process of carrying out a strategic audit requires managers to stand back from the day-to-day activities and take stock of the "resource capabilities" of the business. For small firms there is often little time (or so it seems) to be able to divert attention from the daily routine to consider what the corporate strengths and weaknesses are. It is best, therefore, to share out the task and carry out the activity in small blocks of time. A practical way of starting is on the publication of the annual accounts, for these can provide invaluable insights into the state of the busi-

> **The process of carrying out a strategic audit requires managers to stand back from the day-to-day activities and take stock of the "resource capabilities" of the business.**

ness. In particular they give a view of the financial strengths and weaknesses of the company, which are easily quantified and bench-marked against other firms in the same industry sector. Also they indicate the scope of the firm's ability to carry out strategic investment. Accounting information should also provide the board with the means to make an intelligent interpretation of the operational issues which are affecting overall results.

The second area to tackle is the assessment of the product range. A statement is needed identifying the stage each product has reached in its life cycle and a clear description of the market segments being penetrated. Data about sales trends and about the profiles of one's customers are invaluable. Similarly, the information needed for a human resource audit should be available and in a form which facilitates a positive discussion. In carrying out an evaluation of a company's present position, it is useful to keep at the forefront of the discussion two key inter-related questions:

1. What is our business? This is potentially a dangerous question, since the answer may be unhelpful or even lead to a misguided strategy (the elevator manufacturer who believes the firm is in the people–moving business may decide to buy a fleet of cabs). A better question is:

---

What do our skills, our assets, our products, and services enable us to do? In other words, what markets are we experienced in?

---

2. What do we do that is the basis of some competitive advantage for us and which enables us to "make money?"

The production of a product/market matrix can be a helpful trigger in this discussion, especially if associated with costing information. This identifies gaps in the product range or in the markets served and gives clues as to the relative contributions made by each component in the matrix.

# WHAT WILL HAPPEN IF WE DO NOTHING?

It is sometimes necessary to paint a vision of commercial hell – the situation which might arise if circumstances change outside the firm and no positive action is taken within to offset them. In terms of motivation, this might not always be the most effective driver, but the question needs to be asked anyway: Can we prosper long term if no changes are made to the way we operate? At a more positive level, the difference between an uninteresting future (as suggested by an "if it ain't broke, don't fix it" strategy) and a challenging vision to which everyone can subscribe, has a much more powerful stimulus to action. The size of the planning gap must be measured and communicated

> **It is sometimes necessary to paint a vision of commercial hell – the situation which might arise if circumstances change outside the firm and no positive action is taken within to offset them.**
>
> **The size of the planning gap must be measured and communicated.**

# HOW MIGHT THE BUSINESS ENVIRONMENT CHANGE?

There is no limit to the amount of information that a firm can collect about the environments in which it is operating. For the smaller firm which has to be selective, the task must be assigned to differing functions, with periodic but regular reviews of findings. To some extent this process is akin to the worlds of political and military intelligence: there are times when the information gathered has no meaning or significance on its own, but when connected to other facts, may reveal a trend of some importance. A checklist of external information could be inexhaustive, but in the *essential list*, the following aspects must be kept under constant watch:

---

### ♦ ASPECTS TO WATCH ♦

- Economic trends in all the markets in which the firm operates, or might operate.
- Social trends, especially if the product or service is socially sensitive.
- Technological change and advances within the industrial/commercial sectors of the firm.
- What the competition is doing – financially, technologically, and in marketing terms – pricing, advertising, promotion, selling effort, and so on: "Know your enemy."

---

A more subtle question in this area is: What *might* happen to upset | **"Know your enemy."**
our plans? There is no easy way of identifying the answer to this, but we have seen how using scenarios can give food for thought and often prepare a firm for the unthinkable.

# SELECTING STRATEGIC OPTIONS

The simplest question is: What could we do to achieve our objectives? This should only be asked after the stages described above have been systematically reviewed. The options need to be reviewed bearing in mind that strategies can be *defensive* or *aggressive*. A defensive strategy keeps out competition by making the cost of entry too high and giving one a strong competitive advantage in the marketplace. It secures the profitability of the firm and enables it to grow without undue risk. Aggressive strategies, on the other hand, take the market by the throat and shake up the rules of the game. The generic strategic options will be considered with these two stances in mind. In the words of Hamel and Prahalad:

*What is Strategy? centers on three elements:*

- *the fit between a company and its environment.*
- *allocation of resources among competing investment opportunities.*
- *long-term perspective in which "patient money" figures predominantly. Strategic investments require a large and pre-emptive commitment of resources, as well as a distant return and substantial risk.*
- *This is not wrong – just unbalanced. An alternative . . . is the concept of stretch supplementing fit; leveraging resources is as important as allocating them; long-term has as much to do with consistency of effort and purpose as with patient money and appetite for risk.*

The basic strategic options that might be pursued were discussed in Chapter 3. Every idea which is forthcoming should be tested against the following eight criteria:

1 How quickly would it take to get the strategy up and running?
2 How much of the planning gap will it fill?
3 Do we have the resources (money, people, technology, capacity) to make it happen?

If not, how do we get them? The actual size of the problem may not be precisely assessable at this stage, but as in any project, the aims of the feasibility study and other work at the pre-tender phase are designed to get a good idea of the likely asset needs.

4 If we do it, what will the competition do? How fast will they react?
5 Will the shareholders approve it? Can we sell the strategy to them? Or do we keep it secret for the time being, so as not to alert competitors to our plans?
6 What will our suppliers, customers, unions, and the banks think?
7 What are the risks to the strategy? This is probably the question on which most time should be spent, since it is too easy to be

carried away by the excitement of doing something new and ignoring the possibility that things could (can, and do!) go wrong. If the company has a resident pessimist, they are likely to dream up any number of possible depressing scenarios, but it is the *probability* of something going wrong which is important. If necessary, ask the strategic planning team to put their own risk rating on it, remembering the dictums:

---

**The greater the potential reward, the greater the risk.**

---

**Risk increases the further away you go from your core business.**

---

8 What level of risk are we prepared to tolerate? This should be related to commercial risk, not financial risk, which will be discussed separately. If a strategic move requires a high level of debt financing (simply because of its size), the first question to discuss is whether the new level of gearing (debt to equity capital) is, in itself, too risky. Similarly, if the strategy involves foreign exchange risk of any kind, the implications of dealing across financial frontiers must be tackled.

# STRATEGIC FILTERING

The selection of a strategy from a list of possibles which have passed the tests described above, takes time and not inconsiderable effort. The three aspects to evaluate are:

1 The costs of the investment have to be assembled in as much detail as possible. In the construction industry, quantity surveyors and estimators have the specialist skills to carry out this work, but for other firms the expertise is not to hand. The point has been made that to underestimate the **The point has been made that to underestimate the investment cost is one way of ensuring that the project is accepted. It is also a sure way of ruining the firm.**

investment cost is one way of ensuring that the project is accepted. It is also a sure way of ruining the firm.

2 What are the revenue streams from the strategy – in crude terms, what volumes are likely to be sold, at what prices, and with what levels of selling and promotional support? How will they build up over time? This stage alone is time-consuming and often highly subjective, unless an acquisition is contemplated, in which case historical evidence is available as a basis. If it is planned to invade a new market or develop a new product or service, much less will be known and test marketing is not always possible. Euro Disney's plans were based on their American and Japanese experiences and there were no other meaningful yardsticks.

3 Given the expected volume of business and the nature of the capital investment, what will the operating costs be? With investments where there is a degree of flexibility in the capital intensity of the project, several options can be presented and each will have a different cost structure. For example, it may be possible to invest in a project employing extensively CAM (computer-aided manufacture) techniques and equipment. This will increase the capital cost of the project. However, the operating costs thereafter should be lower and the associated tax allowances higher, giving a very different cash flow profile and a different IRR as a result.

# TAKING THE DECISION

The view is often held that Japanese companies are so logical in the evaluation of projects that at the end only one option is left, so no actual decision needs to be taken. Where a decision has to be taken, the financial evidence must form a great part in making up the mind of the board, but even then – although the numbers seem to make sense and the risks are acceptable – time must be taken to "chew over the cud," asking this question of the proposition:

> **Does it make sense in our context, and in the light of our own values and vision and do we have the resources (or can we "leverage" them)?**

Consider this quotation:

*Successful business strategies result not from rigorous analysis but from a particular state of mind . . . insight and a consequent drive for achievement, often amounting to a sense of mission, fuel a thought process that is basically creative and intuitive rather than rational. Strategists do not reject analysis. Indeed they can hardly do without it. But they use it only to stimulate the creative process, to test the ideas that emerge, to whizz-kid ideas that might otherwise never be implemented properly. Great strategies . . . call for technical mastery in the working out but originate in insights that are beyond the reach of conscious analysis.*

(Ohmae 1982)

# GAINING COMMITMENT

It is a truism to assert that people make strategy happen and no matter how long and hard senior managers work on the strategic investment plan, if there is no commitment by the staff who have to make it happen, then at best the result will be very unsatisfactory. Leadership covers several elements in the process:

- Setting out the vision and enthusing others with its merits. The phrase "developing a shared vision" means making sure that those who have the power to make things happen are all signed up to it; they believe it and want it to happen. The means of achieving this end are various but it is noticeable that the common elements include a high level and frequency of two-way communications, of discussion and of debate, both in formal settings and informally.

- The leader drives the process and continually pesters, nags and worries, terrier like, to make certain that the intelligence is being gathered, and that analysis and evaluation are being taken seriously.

- Leadership in business is also about questioning conventional wisdom and challenging cherished beliefs and attitudes. The damn-fool question may be the best question to ask.

- A simple but often missed element is the extent to which everyone involved actually understands the significance of the statistics (both financial and otherwise) which are inevitably thrown about in capital investment debates. A recent survey made by the authors among a group of international, senior level executives found that 60 percent admitted to having little or no theoretical knowledge of investment appraisal techniques. It is worth asking whether all involved in the decision are fully comfortable with the numbers, for too often approval is given rather than admission to a failure to understand.

Leadership in business these days is not easy and those who find they are forced to lead the process of *strategic change* need to be aware of the techniques and methodologies of change before it becomes necessary. It will be too late once the process has started.

# MOTIVATING

The vital component in leading strategic change is motivation. Recently a case came to our notice about a company where all the managers had attended a corporate strategy meeting at which they were addressed by the chief executive. The presentation was intended as a way of telling everyone what the "plan" was. Two senior managers who had been in the audience were discussing the presentation and one of them said: "The problem was, nobody in the room believed him."

You may draw your own conclusions from this, but it does reinforce the view that managers can be a cynical bunch if what they are hearing does not make sense in their own context. Of course managers can be wrong, but unless they can be persuaded otherwise, motivating them is going to be very tough. Winning the hearts and minds of those who have to implement the strategy requires more than edicts and exhortation. Leadership styles are many and various, but it takes exceptionally fine rhetoric to motivate an intelligent and experienced workforce. Again anyone who has to drive through a strategic change programme should be cognizant of the theories and methods of motivation.

## Making it happen

To implement effectively a strategic investment decision, it is vital that a project team be appointed with the specific remit of turning the plan into reality. In the building and construction industries the site manager has this task and the equivalent should be in place whenever a strategic investment plan is agreed. The appointment of the key drivers must be made immediately and they must be given full authority and responsibility for seeing through the project. In all but the smallest moves, the individuals appointed should be taken off other work, for the project should be the team's sole task and. As well as being given a full and explicit briefing they must provide regular feedback reports on timing, cost and expected completion dates.

# POST-COMPLETION AUDIT

Always insist that a comparison be made after the event. With strategic decisions it is worth reviewing what has actually happened on an annual basis for several years after the investment was first proposed. This provides useful experience for future investment decisions and also enables corrective action to be taken if the results that were originally planned are not materializing. Euro Disney's poor early attendances caused a major shift in policy by, for example, permitting the sale of alcoholic drinks in the Park – previously unthinkable.

# HOW TO GET THE PROJECT ACCEPTED

We often hear the complaint that "our project proposals get turned down." Usually the failure is not because the idea is commercially flawed, but because the idea does not stand up to the rigorous testing which most firms apply to capital investment plans. Remember that accountants and bankers work to the principle of prudence which forces an inspection of every aspect of a proposition, testing all the time for consistency and logic. The five aspects which must add up, logically as well as arithmetically, are:

- sales volume
- project operating costs
- capital costs
- hurdle rates
- timing

## Sales volume

Sales volume forecasts are the easiest target, since it is actually difficult to prove what sales are going to be. The sales numbers in the proposal have to be backed by evidence (trends, sales leads, prospects, etc.) and conviction that they are achievable.

## Project operating costs

The costs of the project can often be understated – include everything and be cautious.

**The costs of the project can often be understated – include everything and be cautious.**

## Capital cost

Investments often cost more than originally envisaged. Accountants know that these costs can easily get out of control and tend to view with a degree of skepticism most investment proposals of a complex nature which appear very rosy. The cost overruns on the Channel Tunnel are a cautionary tale for all. Be able to prove the cost, remembering that even if it is a straight simple purchase, getting the project up and running and conforming with one's own systems and standards will cost a great deal in addition. The cost of buying a business does not end with acquiring the keys of the building – this is when the real, hidden costs start.

## Hurdle rates

Assuming that the raw data themselves are acceptable, unless the IRR and DCF calculations meet or exceed the company's expectations then the project will founder unless there are exceptionally strong arguments *beyond the project* which counterbalance them. For example, to relocate may be necessary strategically – to take advantage of tax breaks, or for image reasons, for instance – but the costs of setting up a new headquarters may not be justifiable on a purely discounted return basis. To get the proposal accepted the final arbitrating body first has to be convinced that a lower return should be applied to a project of this nature and, second, that failure to act will have "knock-on-effect" in other parts of the firm. These items are difficult to quantify, but surveys can sometimes indicate what might happen – back to the "do nothing" scenario described earlier.

## Timing

The "hockey stick" plan has already been described, where everything appears to come out right in the last year. Evaluators of investment proposals are aware of this feature and will question its validity.

It will be appreciated, of course, knowing that money has a time value, that this kind of cash flow pattern actually leads to a lower discounted return than the straight line forecast. So smarter projections weight the positive cash flows in the early years. The effect on the return is thus enhanced, increasing the chances of demonstrating an acceptable project. This ploy is also well known and likely to be scrutinized closely. Many projects are completed on time and the use of such techniques as *Critical Path Analysis* help to reduce the chance of timing miscalculations. However, as with Eurotunnel, the timing delays could have forced an abandonment of the project at various stages in its construction and were far beyond the estimates in the original prospectus.

The golden rule is to assume the worst and if things get out of hand so badly there has to be a point at which the project – or even the strategy itself – has to be abandoned.

The "abandonment decision" is the most difficult to take for it is an admission that the calculations

**The golden rule is to assume the worst and if things get out of hand so badly there has to be a point at which the project – or even the strategy itself – has to be abandoned.**

202

were inaccurate. It is also an admission that money has in effect been thrown away. Nevertheless, the limits of time and money should always be included in the original calculations, just in case.

# CASE STUDY

## Merrydown

Merrydown plc is a small company, based in the South of England, which manufactures and sells cider. Cider is a popular drink in the UK, accounting for about 5 percent of all units of alcohol consumed, and is a "natural" product made from apples and little else. The market volume is approaching 500 million litres a year and growing.

The market is dominated by two large companies (H. P. Bulmer and Taunton Cider), together accounting for over 80 percent of the total. Merrydown's share is some 5 percent. Cider is sold through supermarket chains, pubs and off licences (liqor stores), most of which are owned, in the UK, by large companies.

Merrydown's shares are quoted on the London Stock Exchange and for a time the firm's price/earnings ratio comfortably exceeded the average for the drinks sector. Being a small player, with only some two hundred employees, it has always specialized in the premium end of the market, making an expensive, relatively strong cider, using only apples from English orchards.

Recognizing the need to find alternative ways of growing, Merrydown began to widen its product portfolio with the introduction of so-called "adult soft drinks." Coincidentally, the competitive position began to be eroded by two "forces" – the power of the customers and of the competition. The company was forced to respond by cutting its prices. In the year ending March 31 1992, the company's sales revenues amounted to £17.3m, with an aftertax profit of £1.2m, on total assets of £18.7m and an equity capital base of £10.5m.

At the end of 1992 Merrydown had the opportunity to acquire the manufacturing, distribution and selling rights for two adult soft drink brands called PLJ ( pure lemon juice) and Schloer (a premium priced sparkling fruit juice drink, sold in various flavors) from

SmithKline Beecham plc. The price was for an aggregate minimum cash consideration of £8,255,000, of which £4,350,000 was payable on completion. No tangible fixed assets or liabilities were to be included, so that in effect Merrydown was acquiring two brand names. To make the purchase possible Merrydown decided to raise additional equity capital, since its own liquid funds were minimal and its debt levels were considered to be "high enough."

The rationale for the purchase was explained in the share offer document:

> The Directors' strategy is to maintain and capitalise on the Group's well-established position as a manufacturer of premium quality ciders and to continue to expand its portfolio into other growth sectors of the drinks market. The Directors believe that both cider and adult non-alcoholic drinks are growth sectors – sales of both have proved to be resilient in the current recessionary climate.
>
> The proposed acquisition . . . represents an unique and attractive opportunity for Merrydown to expand the Group's portfolio of adult non-alcoholic drinks.
>
> Both Schloer and PLJ can be produced predominantly using the Group's existing manufacturing and bottling facilities and will be distributed and sold mainly using existing sales and distribution capabilities. As a result, the Directors expect to achieve a significant contribution to the Group's profits from sales (of the new products) and to benefit from material economies of scale in the areas of sales and distribution, across the range of its drinks brands.
>
> Your Directors also believe that within Merrydown there is considerable scope, in particular, for the growth and development of the Schloer brand. We will explore opportunities for the brand – especially for new channels of distribution, new flavours and new bottle sizes – and the possibility of its promotion as a summer-time as well as a winter-time drink.

The offer document stated that 40 percent of Schloer's sales were in the months of November and December, whereas cider sales peak in the summer months. Accounting data relating to the two products show the following:

| Year ending December 31 1991 | | |
| --- | --- | --- |
| | Schloer | PLJ |
| | £000 | £000 |
| Net sales | 6,579 | 817 |
| Less: Prime costs, advertising, marketing, variable factory overheads | 3,929 | 402 |
| Contribution to general overheads | 2,650 | 415 |

The two previous years' figures were given, showing that there was a declining trend in sales of Schloer, but the "Directors are confident . . . that the decline can be reversed."

The deal went through early in 1993 and was followed by two very difficult years with aggressive competition, pressure from customers, and two average summers. It is not possible to estimate the final out-turn at the time of writing, but the case illustrates many of the points that this book has been discussing.

Think about these questions, some of which are general, and some specific to the case:

- What can your strategy be if the competition and your customers are much bigger than you?
- If you had been a director of Merrydown in 1992 what would your strategy have been?
- Is it wise to buy intangible assets, such as brand names? If so, at what price?
- Given the opportunity to buy these two brand names (and no other assets) would you have taken it?
- What were the risks?
- Did it make economic sense?

- Was there any dependence on a synergistic effect or were they simply leveraging existing resources?
- Was the size of the deal too big for the company?
- Does the deal feel right or not?
- Was there likely to be any impact on the staff at Merrydown?

# CONCLUSION

Business is about risk – not reckless gambling – and taking a cold look into the future to assess the prospects of increasing wealth more than you would if resources were locked away in a bank vault.

The art of investment appraisal is in the use of data and intelligence about the business and its environment. The prize goes to those who interpret these elements in the most intelligent and imaginative way and have the drive and commitment to make it happen. If business was able to improve the odds – improve the chances of success and reduce the chances of poor investment decisions by even a small margin – then the incremental wealth created would be truly significant. It would be great if it happened.

On a note for personal action, if you find yourself involved in strategic investment decisions, bear in mind the frameworks that have been discussed in these pages – continually evaluate and assess whether what is proposed is the best possible course of action to lead to the desired result. Finally, keep an eye on the big stories of our time and see how they develop – Shell's Troll field, Siemen's new plant in the North of England, Euro Disney, and some lesser but no less important stories for those involved. What about Le Lièvre Blanc? It's doing very nicely – all they need are a few winters with lots of snow.

# BIBLIOGRAPHY

◆

Ansoff, Igor (1984) *Implementing Strategic Management*, Prentice Hall.

Brealey, Richard and Myers, S. (1992) *Principles of Corporate Finance*, McGraw Hill.

Cooke, S. and Slack, N. (1991) *Making Management Decisions*, Prentice Hall.

Goold, M. and Campbell, A. (1987). *Strategies and Styles*, Basil Blackwell.

Gouillart, F. and Kelly, J. (1995) *Transforming the Organisation*, McGraw Hill.

Grundy, A.N. (1992) *Corporate Strategy and Financial Decisions*, Kogan Page.

Hamel, G. and Prahalad, C.K. (1994) *Competing for the Future*, Harvard Business School Press.

Johnson, Gerry and Scholes, Kevan (1993) *Exploring Corporate Strategy*, Prentice Hall.

Kay, J. (1993) *Foundations of Corporate Success: How Business Strategies Add Value*, Oxford University Press.

Koch, Richard (1993) *The Financial Times Guide to Strategy*, Pitman.

Mills, Roger W. (1994) *Finance, Strategy and Strategic Value Analysis*, Mars Business Associates.

Ohmae, Kenichi (1982) *The Mind of the Strategist*, McGraw Hill.

Pascale, Richard (1991) *Managing on the Edge*, Penguin.

Peters, T. and Waterman, R. (1982) *In Search of Excellence*, Harper & Row.

Porter, Michael (1985) *Competitive Advantage*, Free Press.

Rappaport, Alfred (1986) *Creating Shareholder Value: The New Standard for Business Performance*, Free Press.

Slatter, Stuart (1992) *Gambling on Growth*, John Wiley & Sons.

Taylor, Bernard (1994) *Successful Change Strategies*, Institute of Directors.

Tomkins, C. (1991) *Corporate Resource Allocation*, Basil Blackwell.

Ward, Keith (1992) *Strategic Management Accounting*, Butterworth Heinemann.

Whittington, Richard (1993) *What is Strategy and Does It Matter?*, Routledge.

# INDEX

◆

## Dear Pitman Publishing Customer

## We are delighted to announce a special free service for all of our customers.

Simply complete this form and return it to the FREEPOST address overleaf to receive:

- Free Customer Newsletter
- Free Information Service
- Exclusive Customer Offers – which have included free software, videos and relevant products
- Opportunity to take part in product development sessions
- The chance for you to write about your own business experience and become one of our respected authors

Fill this in now and return it to us (no stamp needed in the UK) to join our customer information service.

Name: _____ Position: _____

Company/Organisation: _____

Address (including postcode): _____

Country: _____

Telephone: _____ Fax: _____

Nature of business: _____

Title of book purchased: _____

ISBN (printed on back cover): [0] [2] [7] [3] [ ] [ ] [ ] [ ] [ ]

Comments: _____

--------------------------- **Fold Here Then Staple Once** ---------------------------

We would be very grateful if you could answer these questions to help us with market research.

**1 Where/How did you hear of this book?**
- [ ] in a bookshop
- [ ] in a magazine/newspaper (please state which): _____
- [ ] information through the post
- [ ] recommendation from a colleague
- [ ] other (please state which): _____

**2 Where did you buy this book?**
- [ ] Direct from Pitman Publishing
- [ ] From a bookclub
- [ ] From a bookshop (state which) _____

**3 Which newspaper(s)/magazine(s) do you read regularly?**
_____

**4 When buying a business book which factors influence you most?**
(Please rank in order)
- [ ] recommendation from a colleague
- [ ] price
- [ ] content
- [ ] recommendation in a bookshop
- [ ] author
- [ ] publisher
- [ ] title
- [ ] other(s): _____

**5 Is this book a**
- [ ] personal purchase?
- [ ] company purchase ?

**6 Would you be prepared to spend a few minutes talking to our customer services staff to help with product development?**
- [ ] yes
- [ ] no

### The Business Publisher

Written for managers competing in today's tough business world, our books will give you a competitive edge by showing you how to:

- increase quality, efficiency and productivity throughout your organisation
- use both proven and innovative management techniques
- improve your management skills and those of your staff
- implement winning customer strategies

In short they provide concise, practical information that you can use every day to manage more effectively

---

Free Information Service
Pitman Professional Publishing
FREEPOST
128 Long Acre
LONDON
WC2E 9BR, UK

No stamp
necessary
in the UK